TREATISE ON RHETORICAL INVENTION

AND

TREATISE ON TOPICS

BY MARCUS TULLIUS CICERO

TRANSLATED BY C. D. YONGE

A Digireads.com Book
Digireads.com Publishing

Treatise on Rhetorical Invention and Treatise on Topics
By Marcus Tullius Cicero
Translated by C. D. Yonge
ISBN: 1-4209-3435-X

Please visit *www.digireads.com*

CONTENTS

THE TWO BOOKS WHICH REMAIN OF

THE TREATISE BY M. T. CICERO ON RHETORICAL INVENTION.

* * * * *

BOOK I.

* * * * *

These essays on rhetoric were composed by Cicero when he was about one and twenty years of age, and he mentions them afterwards in his more elaborate treatise *De Oratore*, (Lib. i. c. 2,) as unworthy of his more mature age, and more extended experiences. Quintilian also (III. c. 63,) mentions them as works which Cicero condemned by subsequent writings. This treatise originally consisted of four books, of which only two have come down to us.

I. I HAVE often and deeply resolved this question in my mind, whether fluency of language has been beneficial or injurious to men and to cities, with reference to the cultivation of the highest order of eloquence. For when I consider the disasters of our own republic, and when I call to mind also the ancient calamities of the most important states, I see that it is by no means the most insignificant portion of their distresses which has originated from the conduct of the most eloquent men. But, at the same time, when I set myself to trace back, by the aid of written memorials and documents, affairs which, by reason of their antiquity, are removed back out of the reach of any personal recollection, I perceive also that many cities have been established, many wars extinguished, many most enduring alliances and most holy friendships have been cemented by deliberate wisdom much assisted and facilitated by eloquence. And as I have been, as I say, considering all this for some time, reason itself especially induces me to think that wisdom without eloquence is but of little advantage to states, but that eloquence without wisdom is often most mischievous, and is never advantageous to them.

If then any one, neglecting all the most virtuous and honourable considerations of wisdom and duty, devotes his whole attention to the practice of speaking, that man is training himself to become useless to himself, and a citizen mischievous to his country; but a man who arms himself with eloquence in such a manner as not to oppose the advantage of his country, but to be able to contend in behalf of them, he appears to me to be one who both as a man and a citizen will be of the greatest service to his own and the general interests, and most devoted to his country.

And if we are inclined to consider the origin of this thing which is called eloquence, whether it be a study, or an art, or some peculiar sort of training or some faculty given us by nature, we shall find that it has arisen from most honourable causes, and that it proceeds on the most excellent principles.

II. For there was a time when men wandered at random over the fields, after the fashion of beasts, and supported life on the food of beasts; nor did they do anything by means of the reasoning powers of the mind; but almost everything by bodily strength. No attention was as yet paid to any considerations of the religious reverence due to the gods, or of the duties which are owed to mankind: no one had ever seen any legitimate marriages, no one had beheld any children whose parentage was indubitable; nor had any one any idea what great advantage there might be in a system of equal law. And so, owing to error and ignorance, cupidity, that blind and rash sovereign of the mind, abused its bodily strength, that most pernicious of servants, for the purpose of gratifying itself. At this time then a man, [1] a great and a wise man truly was he, perceived what materials there were, and what great fitness there was in the minds of men for the most important affairs, if any one could only draw it out, and improve it by education. He, laying down a regular system, collected men, who were previously dispersed over the fields and hidden in habitations in the woods into one place, and united them, and leading them on to every useful and honourable pursuit, though, at first, from not being used to it they raised an outcry against it; he gradually, as they became more eager to listen to him on account of his wisdom and eloquence, made them gentle and civilized from having been savage and brutal. And it certainly seems to me that no wisdom which was silent and destitute of skill in speaking could have had such power as to turn men on a sudden from their previous customs, and to lead them to the adoption of a different system of life. And, moreover, after cities had been established how could men possibly have been induced to learn to cultivate integrity, and to maintain justice, and to be accustomed willingly to obey others, and to think it right not only to encounter toil for the sake of the general advantage, but even to run the risk of losing their lives, if men had not been able to persuade them by eloquence of the truth of those principles which they had discovered by philosophy? Undoubtedly no one, if it had not been that he was influenced by dignified and sweet eloquence, would ever have chosen to condescend to appeal to law without violence, when he was the most powerful party of the two as far as strength went; so as to allow himself now to be put on a level with those men among whom he might have been preeminent, and of his own free will to abandon a custom most pleasant to him, and one which by reason of its antiquity had almost the force of nature.

[1] There is much dispute as to who is meant here. Some say Cicero refers to Amphion, some to Orpheus, and some to Mercury; the Romans certainly did attribute the civilization of men to Mercury, as Horace says—

> Qui feros cultus hominum recenti
> Voce formâsti catus I. 9, 2.

And this is how eloquence appears to have originated at first, and to have advanced to greater perfection; and also, afterwards, to have become concerned in the most important transactions of peace and war, to the greatest advantage of mankind? But after that a certain sort of complaisance, a false copyist of virtue, without any consideration for real duty, arrived at some fluency of language, then wickedness, relying on ability, began to overturn cities, and to undermine the principles of human life.

III. And, since we have mentioned the origin, of the good done by eloquence, let us explain also the beginning of this evil.

It appears exceedingly probable to me that was a time when men who were destitute of eloquence and wisdom, were not accustomed to meddle with affairs of state, and when also great and eloquent men were not used to concern themselves about private causes; but, while the most important transactions were managed by the most eminent and able men, I think that there were others also, and those not very incompetent, who attended to the trifling disputes of private individuals; and as in these disputes it often happened that men had recourse to lies, and tried by such means to oppose the truth, constant practice in speaking encouraged audacity, so that it became unavoidable that those other more eminent men should, on account of the injuries sustained by the citizens, resist the audacious and come to the assistance of their own individual friends.

Therefore, as that man had often appeared equal in speaking, and sometimes even superior, who having neglected the study of wisdom, had laboured to acquire nothing except eloquence, it happened that in the judgment of the multitude he appeared a man worthy to conduct even the affairs of the state. And hence it arose, and it is no wonder that it did, when rash and audacious men had seized on the helm of the republic, that great and terrible disasters occurred. Owing to which circumstances, eloquence fell under so much odium and unpopularity that the ablest men, (like men who seek a harbour to escape from some violent tempest) devoted themselves to any quiet pursuit, as a refuge from a life of sedition and tumult. So that other virtuous and honourable pursuits appear to me to have become popular subsequently, from having been cultivated in tranquillity by excellent men; but that this pursuit having been abandoned by most of them, grew out of fashion and obsolete at the very time when it should have been more eagerly retained and more anxiously encouraged and strengthened.

For the more scandalously the temerity and audacity of foolish and worthless men was violating a most honourable and virtuous system, to the excessive injury of the republic, the more studiously did it become others to resist them, and to consult the welfare of the republic.

IV. And this principle which I have just laid down did not escape the notice of Cato, nor of Laelus, nor of their pupil, as I may fairly call him, Africanus, nor of the Gracchi the grandson of Africanus; men in whom there was consummate virtue and authority increased by their consummate virtue and eloquence, which might serve as an ornament to these qualities, and as a protection to the republic. Wherefore, in my opinion at least, men ought not the less to devote themselves to eloquence, although some men both in private and public affairs misuse it in a perverse manner; but I think rather that they should apply themselves to it with the more eagerness, in order to prevent wicked men from getting the greatest power to the exceeding injury of the good, and the common calamity of all men; especially as this is the only thing which is of the greatest influence on all affairs both public and private; and as it is by this same quality that life is rendered safe, and honourable, and illustrious, and pleasant. For it is from this source that the most numerous advantages accrue to the republic, if only it be accompanied by wisdom, that governor of all human affairs. From this source it is that praise and honour and dignity flow towards all those who have acquired it; from this source it is that the most certain and the safest defence is provided for their friends. And, indeed, it appears to me, that it is on this particular that men, who in many points are weaker and lower than the beasts, are especially superior to them, namely, in being able to speak.

Wherefore, that man appears to me to have acquired an excellent endowment, who is superior to other men in that very thing in which men are superior to beasts. And if this art is acquired not by nature only, not by mere practice, but also by a sort of regular system of education, it appears to me not foreign to our purpose to consider what those men say who have left us some precepts on the subject of the attainment of it.

But, before we begin to speak of oratorical precepts, I think we must say something of the nature of the art itself; of its duty, of its end, of its materials, and of its divisions. For when we have ascertained those points, then each man's mind will, with the more ease and readiness, be able to comprehend the system itself, and the path which leads to excellence in it.

V. There is a certain political science which is made up of many and important particulars. A very great and extensive portion of it is artificial eloquence, which men call rhetoric. For we do not agree with those men who think that the knowledge of political science is in no need of and has no connexion with eloquence; and we most widely disagree with those, on the other hand, who think that all political ability Is comprehended under the skill and power of a rhetorician. On which account we will place this oratorical ability in such a class as to assert that it is a part of political science. But the duty of this faculty appears to be to speak in a manner suitable to persuading men; the end of it is to persuade by language. And there is difference between the duty of this faculty and its end; that with respect to the duty we consider what ought to be done; with respect to the end we consider what is suitable to the duty. Just as we say, that it is the duty of a physician to prescribe for a patient in a way calculated to cure him; and that his end is to cure him by his prescriptions. And so we shall understand what we are to call the duty of an orator, and also what we are to call his end; since we shall call that his duty which he ought to do, and we shall term that his end for the sake of which he is bound to do his duty.

We shall call that the material of the art, on which the whole art, and all that ability which is derived from art, turns. Just as if we were to call diseases and wounds the material of medicine, because it is about them that all medical science is concerned. And in like manner, we call those subjects with which oratorical science and ability is conversant the materials of the art of rhetoric. And these subjects some have considered more numerous, and others less so. For Gorgias the Leontine, who is almost the oldest of all rhetoricians, considered that an orator was able to speak in the most excellent manner of all men on every subject. And when he says this he seems to be supplying an infinite and boundless stock of materials to this art. But Aristotle, who of all men has supplied the greatest number of aids and ornaments to this art, thought that the duty of the rhetorician was conversant with three kinds of subjects; with the demonstrative, and the deliberative, and the judicial.

The demonstrative is that which concerns itself with the praise or blame of some particular individual; the deliberative is that which, having its place in discussion and in political debate, comprises a deliberate statement of one's opinion; the judicial is that which, having its place in judicial proceedings, comprehends the topics of accusation and defence; or of demand and refusal. And, as our own opinion at least inclines, the art and ability of the orator must be understood to be conversant with these tripartite materials.

VI For Hermagoras, indeed, appears neither to attend to what he is saying, nor to understand what he is promising, for he divides the materials of an orator into the cause, and the examination. The cause he defines to be a thing which has in itself a controversy of language united with the interposition of certain characters. And that part, we too say, is assigned to the orator, for we give him those three parts which we have already mentioned,—the judicial, the deliberative, and the demonstrative. But the examination he defines to be that thing which has in itself a controversy of language, without the interposition of any particular characters, in this way—"Whether there is anything good besides honesty?"—"Whether the senses may be trusted?"—"What is the shape of the world?"—"What is the size of the sun?" But I imagine that all men can easily see that all such questions are far removed from the business of an orator, for it appears the excess of insanity to attribute those subjects, in which we know that the most sublime genius of philosophers has been exhausted with infinite labour, as if they were inconsiderable matters, to a rhetorician or an orator.

But if Hermagoras himself had had any great acquaintance with these subjects, acquired with long study and training, then it would be supposed that he, from relying on his own knowledge, had laid down some false principles respecting the duty of an orator, and had explained not what his art could effect, but what he himself could do. But as it is, the character of the man is such, that any one would be much more inclined to deny him any knowledge of rhetoric, than to grant him any acquaintance with philosophy. Nor do I say this because the book on the art which he published appears to me to have been written with any particular incorrectness, (for, indeed, he appears to me to have shown very tolerable ingenuity and diligence in arranging topics which he had collected from ancient writings on the subject, and also to have advanced some new theories himself,) but it is the least part of the business of an orator to speak concerning his art, which is what he has done: his business is rather to speak from his art, which is what we all see that this Hermagoras was very little able to do. And so that, indeed, appears to us to be the proper materials of rhetoric, which we have said appeared to be such to Aristotle.

VII. And these are the divisions of it, as numerous writers have laid them down: Invention; Arrangement; Elocution; Memory; Delivery. Invention, is the conceiving of topics either true or probable, which may make one's cause appear probable; Arrangement, is the distribution of the topics which have been thus conceived with regular order; Elocution, is the adaptation of suitable words and sentences to the topics so conceived; Memory, is the lasting sense in the mind of the matters and words corresponding to the reception of these topics. Delivery, is a regulating of the voice and body in a manner suitable to the dignity of the subjects spoken of and of the language employed.

Now, that these matters have been briefly defined, we may postpone to another time those considerations by which we may be able to elucidate the character and the duty and the object of this art; for they would require a very long argument, and they have no very intimate connexion with the definition of the art and the delivery of precepts relating to it. But we consider that the man who writes a treatise on the art of rhetoric ought to write about two other subjects also; namely, about the materials of the art, and about its divisions. And it seems, indeed, that we ought to treat of the materials and divisions of this art at the same time. Wherefore, let us first consider what sort of quality invention ought to be, which is the most important of all the divisions, and which applies to every description of cause in which an orator can be engaged.

VIII. Every subject which contains in itself any controversy existing either in language or in disputation, contains a question either about a fact, or about a name, or about a class, or about an action. Therefore, that investigation out of which a cause arises we call a stating of a case. A stating of a case is the first conflict of causes arising from a repulse of an accusation; in this way. "You did so and so;"—"I did not do so;"—or, "it was lawful for me to do so." When there is a dispute as to the fact, since the cause is confirmed by conjectures, it is called a conjectural statement. But when it is a dispute as to a name, because the force of a name is to be defined by words, it is then styled a definitive statement. But when the thing which is sought to be ascertained is what is the character of the matter under consideration, because it is a dispute about violence, and about the character of the affair, it is called a general statement. But when the cause depends on this circumstance, either that that man does not seem to plead who ought to plead, or that he does not plead with that man with whom he ought to plead, or that he does not plead before the proper people, at the proper time, in accordance with the proper law, urging the proper charge, and demanding the infliction of the proper penalty, then it is called a statement by way of demurrer; because the arguing of the case appears to stand in need of a demurrer and also of some alteration. And some one or other of these sorts of statement must of necessity be incidental to every cause. For if there be any one to which it is not incidental, in that there can be no dispute at all; on which account it has no right even to be considered a cause at all.

And a dispute as to fact may be distributed over every sort of time. For as to what has been done, an inquiry can be instituted in this way—"whether Ulysses slew Ajax;" and as to what is being done, in this way—"whether the people of Tregellae are well affected towards the Roman people;" and as to what is going to happen, in this way—"if we leave Carthage uninjured, whether any inconvenience will accrue to the republic."

It is a dispute about a name, when parties are agreed as to the fact, and when the question is by what name that which has been done is to be designated. In which class of dispute it is inevitable on that account that there should be a dispute as to the name; not because the parties are not agreed about the fact, not because the fact is not notorious, but because that which has been done appears in a different light to different people, and on that account one calls it by one name and another by another. Wherefore, in disputes of this kind the matter must be defined by words, and described briefly; as, for instance, if any one has stolen any sacred vessel from a private place, whether he is to be considered a sacrilegious person, or a simple thief. For when that is inquired into, it is necessary to define both points—what is a thief, and what is a sacrilegious person,—and to show by one's own description that the matter which is under discussion ought to be called by a different name from that which the opposite party apply to it.

IX. The dispute about kind is, when it is agreed both what has been done, and when there is no question as to the name by which it ought to be designated; and nevertheless there is a question of what importance the matter is, and of what sort it is, and altogether of what character it is; in this way,—whether it be just or unjust; whether it be useful or useless; and as to all other circumstances with reference to which there is any question what is the character of that which has been done, without there being any dispute as to its name. Humagoras assigned four divisions to this sort of dispute: the deliberative, the demonstrative, the judicial, and the one relating to facts. And, as it seems to us, this was no ordinary blunder of his, and one which it is incumbent on us to reprove; though we may do so briefly, lest, if we were to pass it over in silence, we might be thought to have had no good reason for abandoning his guidance; or if we were to dwell too long on this point, we might appear to have interposed a delay and an obstacle to the other precepts which we wish to lay down.

If deliberation and demonstration are kinds of causes, then the divisions of any one kind cannot rightly be considered causes; for the same matter may appear to be a class to one person, and a division to another; but it cannot appear both a class and a division to the same person. But deliberation and demonstration are kinds of argument; for either there is no kind of argument at all, or there is the judicial kind alone, or there are all three kinds, the judicial and the demonstrative and the deliberative. Now, to say there is no kind of argument at the same time that he says that there are many arguments, and is giving precepts for them, is foolishness. How, too, is it possible that there should be one kind only, namely the judicial, when deliberation and demonstration in the first place do not resemble one another, and are exceedingly different from the judicial kind, and have each their separate object to which they ought to be referred. It follows, then, that there are three kinds of arguments. Deliberation and demonstration cannot properly be considered divisions of any kind of argument. He was wrong, therefore, when he said that they were divisions of a general statement of the case.

X. But if they cannot properly be considered divisions of a kind of argument, much less can they properly be considered divisions of a division of an argument. But all statement of the case is a division of an argument. For the argument is not adapted to the statement of the case, but the statement of the case is adapted to the argument. But demonstration and deliberation cannot be properly considered divisions of a kind of argument, because they are separate kinds of arguments themselves. Much less can they properly be considered divisions of that division, as he calls them. In the next place, if the statement of the case, both itself as a whole; and also any portion of that statement, is a repelling of an accusation, then that which is not a repelling of an accusation is neither a statement of a case, nor a portion of a statement of a case; but if that which is not a repelling of an attack is not a statement of a case, nor a portion of a statement of a case, then deliberation and demonstration are neither a statement of a case, nor a portion of a statement of a case. If, therefore, a statement of a case, whether it be the whole statement or some portion of it, be a repelling of an accusation, then deliberation and demonstration are neither a statement of a case, nor any portion of such statement. But he himself asserts that it is a repelling of an accusation. He must therefore assert also that demonstration and deliberation are neither a statement of a case, nor a portion of such a statement. And he will be pressed by the same argument whether he calls the statement of a case the original assertion of his cause by the accuser, or the first speech in answer to such accusation by the advocate of the defence. For all the same difficulties will attend him in either case.

In the next place a conjectural argument cannot, as to the same portion of it, be at the same time both a conjectural one and a definitive one. Again, a definitive argument cannot, as to the same portion of it, be at the same time both a definitive argument and one in the form and character of a demurrer. And altogether, no statement of a case, and no portion of such a statement, can at one and the same time both have its own proper force and also contain the force of another kind of argument. Because each kind of argument is considered simply by its own merits, and according to its own nature; and if any other kind be united with it, then it is the number of statements of a case that is doubled, and not the power of the statement that is increased.

But a deliberative argument, both as to the same portion of it and also at the same time, very frequently has a statement of its case both conjectural, and general, and definitive, and in the nature of a demurrer; and at times it contains only one statement, and at times it contains many such. Therefore it is not itself a statement of the case, nor a division of such statement: and the same thing must be the case with respect to demonstration. These, then, as I have said before, must be considered kinds of argument, and not divisions of any statement of the subject.

XI. This statement of the case then, which we call the general one, appears to us to have two divisions,—one judicial and one relating to matters of fact. The judicial one is that in which the nature of right and wrong, or the principles of reward and punishment, are inquired into. The one relating to matters of fact is that in which the thing taken into consideration is what is the law according to civil precedent, and according to equity; and that is the department in which lawyers are considered by us to be especially concerned.

And the judicial kind is itself also distributed under two divisions,—one absolute, and one which takes in something besides as an addition, and which may be called assumptive. The absolute division is that which of itself contains in itself an inquiry into right and wrong. The assumptive one is that which of itself supplies no firm ground for objection, but which takes to itself some topics for defence derived from extraneous circumstances. And its divisions are four,—concession, removal of the accusation from oneself, a retorting of the accusation, and comparison. Concession when the person on his trial does not defend the deed that has been done, but entreats to be pardoned for it: and this again is divided into two parts,—purgation and deprecation. Purgation is when the fact is admitted, but when the guilt of the fact is sought to be done away. And this may be on three grounds,—of ignorance, of accident, or of necessity. Deprecation is when the person on his trial confesses that he has done wrong, and that he has done wrong on purpose, and nevertheless entreats to be pardoned. But this kind of address can be used but very rarely.

Removal of the accusation from oneself is when the person on his trial endeavours by force of argument and by influence to remove the charge which is brought against him from himself to another, so that it may not fix him himself with any guilt at all. And that can be done in two ways,—if either the cause of the deed, or the deed itself, is attributed to another. The cause is attributed to another when it is said that the deed was done in consequence of the power and influence of another; but the deed itself is attributed to another when it is said that another either might have done it, or ought to have done it. The retorting of an accusation takes place when what is done is said to have been lawfully done because another had previously provoked the doer wrongfully. Comparison is, when it is argued that some other action has been a right or an advantageous one, and then it is contended that this deed which is now impeached was committed in order to facilitate the accomplishment of that useful action.

In the fourth kind of statement of a case, which we call the one which assumes the character of a demurrer, that sort of statement contains a dispute, in which an inquiry is opened who ought to be the accuser or pleader, or against whom, or in what manner, or before whom, or under what law, or at what time the accusation ought to be brought forward; or when something is urged generally tending to alter the nature of, or to invalidate the whole accusation. Of this kind of statement of a case Hermagoras is considered the inventor: not that many of the ancient orators have not frequently employed it, but because former writers on the subject have not taken any notice of it, and have not entered it among the number of statements of cases. But since it has been thus invented by Hermagoras, many people have found fault with it, whom we considered not so much to be deceived by ignorance (for indeed the matter is plain enough) as to be hindered from admitting the truth by some envy or fondness for detraction.

XII. We have now then mentioned the different kinds of statements of cases, and their several divisions. But we think that we shall be able more conveniently to give instances of each kind, when we are furnishing a store of arguments for each kind. For so the system of arguing will be more clear, when it can be at once applied both to the general classification and to the particular instance.

When the statement of the case is once ascertained, then it is proper at once to consider whether the argument be a simple or a complex one, and if it be a complex one, whether it is made up of many subjects of inquiry, or of some comparison. That is a simple statement which contains in itself one plain question, in this way—"Shall we declare war against the Corinthians, or not?" That is a complex statement consisting of several questions in which many inquiries are made, in this way.—"Whether Carthage shall be destroyed, or whether it shall be restored to the Carthaginians, or whether a colony shall be led thither." Comparison is a statement in which inquiry is raised in the way of contest, which course is more preferable, or which is the most preferable course of all, in this way.—"Whether we had better send an army into Macedonia against Philip, to serve as an assistance to our allies, or whether we had better retain it in Italy, in order that we may have as numerous forces as possible to oppose to Hannibal." In the next place, we must consider whether the dispute turns on general reasoning, or on written documents, for a controversy with respect to written documents, is one which arises out of the nature of the writing.

XIII And of that there are five kinds which have been separated from statements of cases. For when the language of the writing appears to be at variance with the intention of the writer, then two laws or more seem to differ from one another, and then, too, that which has been written appears to signify two things or more. Then also, from that which is written, something else appears to be discovered also, which is not written, and also the effect of the expressions used is inquired into, as if it were in the definitive statement of the case, in which it has been placed. Wherefore, the first kind is that concerning the written document and the intention of it; the second arises from the laws which are contrary to one another, the third is ambiguous, the fourth is argumentative, the fifth we call definitive.

But reason applies when the whole of the inquiry does not turn on the writing, but on some arguing concerning the writing. But, then, when the kind of argument has been duly considered, and when the statement of the case has been fully understood; when you have become aware whether it is simple or complex, and when you have ascertained whether the question turns on the letter of the writing or on general reasoning; then it is necessary to see what is the question, what is the reasoning, what is the system of examining into the excuses alleged, what means there are of establishing one's own allegations; and all these topics must be derived from the original statement of the case. What I call "the question" is the dispute which arises from the conflict of the two statements in this way. "You have not done this lawfully;" "I have done it lawfully." And this is the conflict of arguments, and on this the statement of the case hinges. It arises, therefore, from that kind of dispute which we call "the question," in this way:—"Whether he did so and so lawfully." The reasoning is that which embraces the whole cause; and if that be taken away, then there is no dispute remaining behind in the cause. In this way, in order that for the sake of explaining myself more clearly, I may content myself with an easy and often quoted instance. If Orestes be accused of matricide, unless he says this, "I did it rightfully, for she had murdered my father," he has no defence at all. And if his defence be taken away, then all dispute is taken away also. The principle of his argument then is that she murdered Agamemnon. The examination of this defence is then a dispute which arises out of the attempts to invalidate or to establish this argument. For the argument itself may be considered sufficiently explained, since we dwelt upon it a little while ago. "For she," says he, "had murdered my father." "But," says the adversary, "for all that it was not right for your mother to be put to death by you who were her son; for her act might have been punished without your being guilty of wickedness."

XIV. From this mode of bringing forward evidence, arises that last kind of dispute which we call the judication, or examination of the excuses alleged. And that is of this kind: whether it was right that his mother should be put to death by Orestes, because she had put to death Orestes's father?

Now proof by testimony is the firmest sort of reasoning that can be used by an advocate in defence, and it is also the best adapted for the examination of any excuse which may be alleged. For instance, if Orestes were inclined to say that the disposition of his mother had been such towards his father, towards himself and his sisters, towards the kingdom, and towards the reputation of his race and family, that her children were of all people in the world the most bound to inflict punishment upon her. And in all other statements or cases, examinations of excuses alleged are found to be carried on in this manner. But in a conjectural statement of a case, because there is no express evidence, for the fact is not admitted at all, the examination of the defence put forward cannot arise from the bringing forward of evidence. Wherefore, it is inevitable that in this case the question and the judication must be the same thing. As "it was done," "it was not done." The question is whether it was done.

But it must invariably happen that there will be the same number of questions, and arguments, and examinations, and evidences employed in a cause, as there are statements of the case or divisions of such statements. When all these things are found in a cause, then at length each separate division of the whole cause must be considered. For it does not seem that those points are necessarily to be first noticed, which have been the first stated; because you must often deduce those arguments which are stated first, at least if you wish them to be exceedingly coherent with one another and to be consistent with the cause, from those arguments which are to be stated subsequently. Wherefore, when the examination of the excuses alleged, and all those arguments which require to be found out for the purpose of such examination have been diligently found out by the rules of art, and handled with due care and deliberation, then at length we may proceed to arrange the remaining portions of our speech. And these portions appear to us to be in all six; the exordium, the relation of the fact, the division of the different circumstances and topics, the bringing forward of evidence, the finding fault with the action which has been done, and the peroration.

At present, since the exordium ought to be the main thing of all, we too will first of all give some precepts to lead to a system of opening a case properly.

XV. An exordium is an address bringing the mind of the hearer into a suitable state to receive the rest of the speech, and that will be effected if it has rendered him well disposed towards the speaker, attentive, and willing to receive information. Wherefore, a man who is desirous to open a cause well, must of necessity be beforehand thoroughly acquainted with the nature and kind of cause which he has to conduct. Now the kinds of causes are five; one honourable, one astonishing, one low, one doubtful, one obscure. The kind of cause which is called honourable, is such an one as the disposition of the hearer favours at once, without waiting to hear our speech. The kind that is astonishing, is that from which the mind of those who are about to hear us has been alienated. The kind which is low, is one which is disregarded by the hearer, or which does not seem likely to be carefully attended to. The kind which is doubtful, is that in which either the examination into the excuses alleged is doubtful, or the cause itself, being partly honourable and partly discreditable; so as to produce partly good-will and partly disinclination. The kind which is obscure, is that in which either the hearers are slow, or in which the cause itself is entangled in a multitude of circumstances hard to be thoroughly acquainted with. Wherefore, since there are so many kinds of causes, it is necessary to open one's case on a very different system in each separate kind. Therefore, the exordium is divided into two portions, first of all a beginning, and secondly language calculated to enable the orator to work his way into the good graces of his hearers. The beginning is an address, in plain words, immediately rendering the hearer well disposed towards one, or inclined to receive information, or attentive. The language calculated to enable the orator to work his way into the good graces of his hearers, is an address which employs a certain dissimulation, and which by a circuitous route as it were obscurely creeps into the affections of the hearer.

In the kind of cause which we have called astonishing, if the hearers be not positively hostile, it will be allowable by the beginning of the speech to endeavour to secure their good-will. But if they be excessively alienated from one, then it will be necessary to have recourse to endeavours to insinuate oneself into their good graces. For if peace and good-will be openly sought for from those who are enemies to one, they not only are not obtained, but the hatred which they bear one is even inflamed and increased. But in the kind of cause which I have called low, for the sake of removing his contempt it will be indispensable to render the hearer attentive. The kind of cause which has been styled doubtful, if it embraces an examination into the excuses alleged, which is also doubtful, must derive its exordium from that very examination; but if it have some things in it of a creditable nature, and some of a discreditable character, then it will be expedient to try and secure the good-will of the hearer, so that the cause may change its appearance, and seem to be an honourable one. But when the kind of cause is the honourable kind, then the exordium may either be passed over altogether, or if it be convenient, we may begin either with a relation of the business in question, or with a statement of the law, or with any other argument which must be brought forward in the course of our speech, and on which we most greatly rely; or if we choose to employ an exordium, then we must avail ourselves of the good-will already existing towards us, in order that that which does exist may be strengthened.

XVI. In the kind of cause which I have called obscure, it will be advisable to render the hearers inclined to receive instruction by a carefully prepared exordium. Now, since it has been already explained what effect is to be sought to be produced by the exordium, it remains for us to show by what arguments all such effects may be produced.

Good-will is produced by dwelling on four topics:—on one derived from our own character, from that of our adversaries, from that of the judges, and from the cause itself. From our own character, if we manage so as to speak of our own actions and services without arrogance; if we refute the charges which have been brought against us, and any other suspicions in the least, discreditable which it may be endeavoured to attach to us; if we dilate upon the inconveniences which have already befallen us, or the difficulties which are still impending over us; if we have recourse to prayers and to humble and suppliant entreaty. From the character of our adversaries, if we are able to bring them either into hatred, or into unpopularity, or into contempt. They will be brought into hatred, if any action of theirs can be adduced which has been lascivious, or arrogant, or cruel, or malignant. They will be made unpopular, if we can dilate upon their violent behaviour, their power, their riches, their numerous kinsmen, their wealth, and their arrogant and intolerable use of all these sources of influence; so that they may appear rather to trust to these circumstances than to the merits of their cause. They will be brought into contempt, if sloth, or negligence, or idleness, or indolent pursuits, or luxurious tranquillity can be alleged against them. Good-will will be procured, derived from the character of the hearers themselves, if exploits are mentioned which have been performed by them with bravery, or wisdom, or humanity; so that no excessive flattery shall appear to be addressed to them; and if it is plainly shown how high and honourable their reputation is, and how anxious is the expectation with which men look for their decision and authority. Or from the circumstances themselves, if we extol our own cause with praises, and disparage that of the opposite party by contemptuous allusions.

But we shall make our hearers attentive, if we show that the things which we are going to say and to speak of are important, and unusual, and incredible; and that they concern either all men, or those who are our present hearers, or some illustrious men, or the immortal gods, or the general interests of the republic. And if we promise that we will in a very short time prove our own cause; and if we explain the whole of the examination into the excuses alleged, or the different examinations, if there be more than one.

We shall render our hearers willing to receive information, if we explain the sum total of the cause with plainness and brevity, that is to say, the point on which the dispute hinges. For when you wish to make a hearer inclined to receive information you must also render him attentive. For he is above all men willing to receive information who is prepared to listen with the greatest attention.

XVII. The next thing which it seems requisite to speak of, is, how topics intended to enable the orator to work his way into the good graces of his hearers ought to be handled. We must then use such a sort of address as that when the kind of cause which we are conducting is that which I have called astonishing; that is to say, as I have stated before, when the disposition of the hearer is adverse to one. And that generally arises from one of three causes: either if there be anything discreditable in the cause itself, or if any such belief appears to have been already instilled into the hearer by those who have spoken previously; or if one is appointed to speak at a time when those who have got to listen to one are wearied with hearing others. For sometimes when one is speaking, the mind of the hearer is alienated from one no less by this circumstance than by the two former.

If the discreditable nature of one's cause excites the ill-will of one's hearers, or if it be desirable to substitute for the man on whom they look unfavourably another man to whom they are attached; or, for the matter they regard with dislike, another matter of which they approve; or if it be desirable to substitute a person for a thing, or a thing for a person, in order that the mind of the hearer may be led away from that which he hates to that which he loves; and if your object is to conceal from view the fact that you are about to defend that person or action which you are supposed to be going to defend; and then, when the hearer has been rendered more propitious, to enter gradually on the defence, and to say that those things at which the opposite party is indignant appear scandalous to you also; and then, when you have propitiated him who is to listen to you, to show that none of all those things at all concern you, and to deny that you are going to say anything whatever respecting the opposite party whether it be good or bad; so as not openly to attack those men who are loved by your hearers, and yet doing it secretly as far as you can to alienate from them the favourable disposition of your hearers; and at the same time to mention the judgment of some other judges in a similar case, or to quote the authority of some others as worthy of imitation; and then to show that it is the very same point, or one very like it, or one of greater or less importance, (as the case may make it expedient,) which is in question at present.

If the speech of your adversaries appears to have made an impression on your hearers, which is a thing which will be very easily ascertained by a man who understands what are the topics by which an impression is made; then it is requisite to promise that you will speak first of all on that point which the opposite party consider their especial stronghold, or else to begin with a reference to what has been said by the adversary, and especially to what he said last; or else to appear to doubt, and to feel some perplexity and astonishment as to what you had best say first, or what argument it is desirable to reply to first—for when a hearer sees the man whom the opposite party believe to be thrown into perplexity by their speech prepared with unshaken firmness to reply to it, he is generally apt to think that he has assented to what has been said without sufficient consideration, rather than that the present speaker is confident without due grounds. But if fatigue has alienated the mind of the hearer from your cause, then it is advantageous to promise to speak more briefly than you had been prepared to speak; and that you will not imitate your adversary.

If the case admit of it, it is not disadvantageous to begin with some new topic, or with some one which may excite laughter; or with some argument which has arisen from the present moment; of which kind are any sudden noise or exclamation; or with something which you have already prepared, which may embrace some apologue, or fable, or other laughable circumstance. Or, if the dignity of the subject shall seem inconsistent with jesting, in that case it is not disadvantageous to throw in something sad, or novel, or terrible. For as satiety of food and disgust is either relieved by some rather bitter taste, or is at times appeased by a sweet taste; so a mind weary with listening is either reinstated in its strength by astonishment, or else is refreshed by laughter.

XVIII. And these are pretty nearly the main things which it appeared desirable to say separately concerning the exordium of a speech, and the topics which an orator should use for the purpose of insinuating himself into the good grace of his hearers. And now it seems desirable to lay down some brief rules which may apply to both in common.

An exordium ought to have a great deal of sententiousness and gravity in it, and altogether to embrace all things which have a reference to dignity; because that is the most desirable effect to be produced which in the greatest degree recommends the speaker to his hearer. It should contain very little brilliancy, or wit, or elegance of expression, because from these qualities there always arises a suspicion of preparation and artificial diligence: and that is an idea which, above all others takes away credit from a speech, and authority from a speaker.

But the following are the most ordinary faults to be found in an exordium, and those it is above all things desirable to avoid. It must not be vulgar, common, easily changed, long, unconnected, borrowed, nor must it violate received rules. What I mean by vulgar, is one which may be so adapted to numerous causes as to appear to suit them all. That is common, which appears to be able to be adapted no less to one side of the argument than to the other. That is easily changed, which with a slight alteration may be advanced by the adversary on the other side of the question. That is long, which is spun out by a superfluity of words or sentences far beyond what is necessary. That is unconnected, which is not derived from the cause itself, and is not joined to the whole speech as a limb is to the body. That is borrowed, which effects some other end than that which the kind of cause under discussion requires; as if a man were to occupy himself in rendering his hearer inclined to receive information, when the cause requires him only to be well disposed towards the speaker: or, if a man uses a formal beginning of a speech, when what the subject requires is an address by which the speaker may insinuate himself into the good graces of his hearer. That is contrary to received rules, which effects no one of those objects for the sake of which the rules concerning exordiums have been handed down. This is the sort of blunder which renders him who hears it neither well disposed to one, nor inclined to receive information, nor attentive; or (and that indeed is the most disastrous effect of all) renders him of a totally contrary disposition. And now we have said enough about the exordium.

XIX. Narration is an explanation of acts that have been done, or of acts as if they have been done. There are three kinds of narration. One kind is that in which the cause itself and the whole principle of the dispute is contained. Another is that in which some digression, unconnected with the immediate argument, is interposed, either for the sake of criminating another, or of instituting a comparison, or of provoking some mirth not altogether unsuitable to the business under discussion, or else for the sake of amplification. The third kind is altogether foreign to civil causes, and is uttered or written for the sake of entertainment, combined with its giving practice, which is not altogether useless. Of this last there are two divisions, the one of which is chiefly conversant about things, and the other about persons. That which is concerned in the discussion and explanation of things has three parts, fable, history, and argument. Fable is that in which statements are expressed which are neither true nor probable, as is this—

"Huge winged snakes, join'd by one common yoke."

History is an account of exploits which have been performed, removed from the recollection of our own age; of which sort is the statement, "Appius declared war against the Carthaginians." Argument is an imaginary case, which still might have happened. Such is this in Terence—

"For after Sosia became a man."

But that sort of narration which is conversant about persons, is of such a sort that in it not only the facts themselves, but also the conversations of the persons concerned and their very minds can be thoroughly seen, in this way—

"And oft he came to me with mournful voice,
What is your aim, your conduct what? Oh why
Do you this youth with these sad arts destroy?
Why does he fall in love? Why seeks he wine,
And why do you from time to time supply
The means for such excess? You study dress
And folly of all kinds; while he, if left
To his own natural bent, is stern and strict,
Almost beyond the claims of virtue."

In this kind of narration there ought to be a great deal of cheerfulness wrought up out of the variety of circumstances; out of the dissimilarity of dispositions; out of gravity, lenity, hope, fear, suspicion, regret, dissimulation, error, pity, the changes of fortune, unexpected disaster, sudden joy, and happy results. But these embellishments may be derived from the precepts which will hereafter be laid down about elocution.

At present it seems best to speak of that kind of narration which contains an explanation of the cause under discussion.

XX. It is desirable then that it should have three qualities; that it should be brief, open, and probable. It will be brief, if the beginning of it is derived from the quarter from which it ought to be; and if it is not endeavoured to be extracted from what has been last said, and if the speaker forbears to enumerate all the parts of a subject of which it is quite sufficient to state the total result;—for it is often sufficient to say what has been done, and there is no necessity for his relating how it was done;—and if the speaker does not in his narration go on at a greater length than there is any occasion for, as far as the mere imparting of knowledge is concerned; and if he does not make a digression to any other topic; and if he states his case in such a way, that sometimes that which has not been said may be understood from that which has been said; and if he passes over not only such topics as may be injurious, but those too which are neither injurious nor profitable; and if he repeats nothing more than once; and if he does not at once begin with that topic which was last mentioned;—and the imitation of brevity takes in many people, so that, when they think that they are being brief, they are exceedingly prolix, while they are taking pains to say many things with brevity, not absolutely to say but few things and no more than are necessary. For to many men a man appears to speak with brevity who says, "I went to the house; I called out the servant; he answered me; I asked for his master; he said that he was not at home." Here, although he could not have enumerated so many particulars more concisely, yet, because it would have been enough to say, "He said that he was not at home," he is prolix on account of the multitude of circumstances which he mentions. Wherefore, in this kind of narration also it is necessary to avoid the imitation of brevity, and we must no less carefully avoid a heap of unnecessary circumstances than a multitude of words.

But a narration will be able to be open, if those actions are explained first which have been done first, and if the order of transactions and times is preserved, so that the things are related as they have been done, or as it shall seem that they may have been done. And in framing this narration it will be proper to take care that nothing be said in a confused or distorted manner; that no digression be made to any other subject; that the affair may not be traced too far back, nor carried too far forward; that nothing be passed over which is connected with the business in hand; and altogether the precepts which have been laid down about brevity, must be attended to in this particular also. For it often happens that the truth is but little understood, more by reason of the prolixity of the speaker, than of the obscurity of the statement. And it is desirable to use clear language, which is a point to be dwelt upon when we come to precepts for elocution.

XXI. A narration will be probable, if in it those characteristics are visible which are usually apparent in truth; if the dignity of the persons mentioned is preserved; if the causes of the actions performed are made plain; if it shall appear that there were facilities for performing them; if the time was suitable; if there was plenty of room; if the place is shown to have been suitable for the transaction which is the subject of the narration; if the whole business, in short, be adapted to the nature of those who plead, and to the reports bruited about among the common people, and to the preconceived opinions of those who hear. And if these principles be observed, the narration will appear like the truth.

But besides all this, it will be necessary to take care that such a narration be not introduced when it will be a hindrance, or when it will be of no advantage; and that it be not related in an unseasonable place, or in a manner which the cause does not require. It is a hindrance, when the very narration of what has been done comes at a time that the hearer has conceived great displeasure at something, which it will be expedient to mitigate by argument, and by pleading the whole cause carefully. And when this is the case, it will be desirable rather to scatter the different portions of the transactions limb by limb as it were over the cause, and, as promptly as may be, to adapt them to each separate argument, in order that there may be a remedy at hand for the wound, and that the defence advanced may at once mitigate the hatred which has arisen.

Again, a narration is of no advantage when, after our case has once been set forth by the opposite party, it is of no importance to relate it a second time or in another manner; or when the whole affair is so clearly comprehended by the hearers, as they believe at least that it can do us no good to give them information respecting it in another fashion. And when this is the case, it is best to abstain from any narration altogether. It is uttered in an unseasonable place, when it is not arranged in that part of the speech in which the case requires it, and concerning this kind of blunder we will speak when we come to mention the arrangement of the speech. For it is the general arrangement of the whole that this affects. It is not related in the manner which the cause requires, when either that point which is advantageous to the opposite party is explained in a clear and elegant manner, or when that which may be of benefit to the speaker is stated in an obscure or careless way. Wherefore, in order that this fault may be avoided, everything ought to be converted by the speaker to the advantage of his own cause by passing over all things which make against it which can be passed over, by touching lightly on those points which are beneficial to the adversary, and by relating those which are advantageous to himself carefully and clearly. And now we seem to have said enough about narration. Let us now pass on in regular order to the arrangement of the different topics.

XXII An arrangement of the subjects to be mentioned in an argument, when properly made, renders the whole oration clear and intelligible. There are two parts in such a division, each of which is especially connected with the opening of the cause, and with the arrangement of the whole discussion. One part is that which points out what are the particulars as to which one is in agreement with the opposite party, and also what remains in dispute; and from this there is a certain definite thing pointed out to the hearer, as that to which he should direct his attention. The other part is that in which the explanation of those matters on which we are about to speak, is briefly arranged and pointed out. And this causes the hearer to retain certain things in his mind, so as to understand that when they have been discussed the speech will be ended. At present it seems desirable to mention briefly how it is proper to use each kind of arrangement. And this arrangement points out what is suitable and what is not suitable; its duty is to turn that which is suitable to the advantage of its own side, in this way—"I agree with the opposite party as to the fact, that a mother has been put to death by her son." Again, on the other side.—"We are both agreed that Agamemnon was slain by Clytaemnestra" For in saying this each speaker has laid down that proposition which was suitable, and nevertheless has consulted the advantage of his own side.

In the next place, what the matter in dispute is must be explained, when we come to mention the examination into the excuses which are alleged. And how that is managed has been already stated.

But the arrangement which embraces the properly distributed explanation of the facts, ought to have brevity, completeness, conciseness. Brevity is when no word is introduced which is not necessary. This is useful in this sort of speaking, because it is desirable to arrest the attention of the hearer by the facts themselves and the real divisions of the case, and not by words or extraneous embellishments of diction. Completeness is that quality by which we embrace every sort of argument which can have any connexion with the case concerning which we have got to speak, and in this division we must take care not to omit any useful topic, not to introduce any such too late, out of its natural place, for that is the most pernicious and discreditable error of all. Conciseness in arrangement is preserved if the general classes of facts are clearly laid down, and are not entangled in a promiscuous manner with the subordinate divisions. For a class is that which embraces many subordinate divisions as, "an animal." A subordinate division is that which is contained in the class as "a horse." But very often the same thing may be a class to one person, and a subordinate division to another. For "man" is a subordinate division of "animal," but a class as to "Theban," or "Trojan."

XXIII. And I have been more careful in laying down this definition, in order that after it has been clearly comprehended with reference to the general arrangement, a conciseness as to classes or genera may be preserved throughout the arrangement. For he who arranges his oration in this manner—"I will prove that by means of the covetousness and audacity and avarice of our adversaries, all sorts of evils have fallen on the republic," fails to perceive that in this arrangement of his, when he intended to mention only classes, he has joined also a mention of a subordinate division. For covetousness is the general class under which all desires are comprehended, and beyond all question avarice is a subordinate division of that class.

We must therefore avoid, after having mentioned a universal class, then, in the same arrangement, to mention along with it any one of its subordinate divisions, as if it were something different and dissimilar. And if there are many subordinate divisions to any particular class, after that has been simply explained in the first arrangement of the oration, it will be more easily and conveniently arranged when we come to the subsequent explanation in the general statement of the case after the division. And this, too, concerns the subject of conciseness, that we should not undertake to prove more things than there is any occasion for, in this way—"I will prove that the opposite party were able to do what we accuse them of, and had the inclination to do it, and did it." It is quite enough to prove that they did it. Or when there is no natural division at all in a cause, and when it is a simple question that is under discussion, though that is a thing which cannot be of frequent occurrence, still we must use careful arrangement. And these other precepts also, with respect to the division of subjects which have no such great connexion with the practice of orators, precepts which come into use in treatises in philosophy, from which we have transferred, hither those which appeared to be suitable to our purpose, of which we found nothing in the other arts. And in all these precepts about the division of our subjects, it will throughout our whole speech be found that every portion of them must be discussed in the same order as that in which it has been originally stated, and then, when everything has been properly explained, let the whole be summed up, and summed up so that nothing be introduced subsequently besides the conclusion. The old man in the Andria of Terence arranges briefly and conveniently the subjects with which he wishes his freedman to become acquainted—

> "And thus the life and habits of my son
> And my designs respecting his career,
> And what I wish your course towards both to be,
> Will be quite plain to you."

And accordingly, as he has proposed in his original arrangement, he proceeds to relate, first the life of his son—

> "For when, O Sosia, he became a man,
> He was allow'd more liberty"

Then comes his own design—

> "And now I take great care"

After that, what he wishes Sosia to do; that he put last in his original arrangement he now mentions last—

"And now the part is yours" ...

As, therefore, in this instance, he came first to the portion which he had mentioned first, and so, when he had discussed them all, made an end of speaking, we too ought to advance to each separate portion of our subject, and when we had finished every part, to sum up. Now it appears desirable to proceed in regular order to lay down some precepts concerning the confirmation of our arguments, as the regular order of the subject requires.

XXIV Confirmation is that by means of which our speech proceeding in argument adds belief, and authority, and corroboration to our cause. As to this part there are certain fixed rules which will be divided among each separate class of causes. But it appeals to be not an inconvenient course to disentangle what is not unlike a wood, or a vast promiscuous miss of materials all jumbled together, and after that to point out how it may be suitable to corroborate each separate kind of cause, after we have drawn all our principles of argumentation from this source. All statements are confirmed by some argument or other, either by that which is derived from persons, or by that which is deduced from circumstances. Now we consider that these different things belong to persons, a name, nature, a way of life, fortune, custom, affection, pursuits, intentions, actions, accidents, orations. A name is that which is given to each separate person, so that each is called by his own proper and fixed appellation. To define nature itself is difficult, but to enumerate those parts of it which we require for the laying down of these precepts is more easy.

And these refer partly to that portion of things which is divine, and partly to that which is mortal. Now of things which are mortal one part is classed among the race of men, and one among the race of brutes: and the race of men is distinguished by sex, whether they be male or female and with respect to their nation, and country, and kindred, and age, with respect to their nation, whether a man be a Greek or a barbarian; with respect to their country, whether a man be an Athenian or a Lacedaemonian; with respect to their kindred, from what ancestors a man is descended, and who are his relations; with respect to his age, whether he is a boy, or a youth, or a full grown man, or an old man. Besides these things, those advantages or disadvantages which come to a man by nature, whether in respect of his mind or his body, are taken into consideration, in this manner:—whether he be strong or weak; whether he be tall or short; whether he be handsome or ugly; whether he be quick in his motions or slow; whether he be clever or stupid; whether he have a good memory, or whether he be forgetful; whether he be courteous, fond of doing kindnesses, modest, patient, or the contrary. And altogether all these things which are considered to be qualities conferred by nature on men's minds or bodies, must be taken into consideration when defining nature. For those qualities which are acquired by industry relate to a man's condition, concerning which we must speak hereafter.

XXV. With reference to a man's way of life it is proper to consider among what men, and in what manner, and according to whose direction he has been brought up; what teachers of the liberal sciences he has had; what admonitors to encourage him to a proper course of life; with what friends he is intimate; in what business, or employment, or gainful pursuit he is occupied; in what manner he manages his estate, and what are his domestic habits. With reference to his fortune we inquire whether he is a slave or a free man; whether he is wealthy or poor; whether he is a private individual or a man in office; if he be in office, whether he has become so properly or improperly; whether he is prosperous, illustrious, or the contrary; what sort of children he has. And if we are inquiring about one who is no longer alive, then we must consider also by what death he died.

But when we speak of a man's habitual condition, we mean his constant and absolute completeness of mind or body, in some particular point—as for instance, his perception of virtue, or of some art, or else some science or other. And we include also some personal advantages not given to him by nature, but procured by study and industry. By affection, we mean a sudden alteration of mind or body, arising from some particular cause, as joy, desire, fear, annoyance, illness, weakness and other things which are found under the same class. But study is the assiduous and earnest application of the mind, applied to some particular object with great good-will, as to philosophy, poetry, geometry, or literature. By counsel, we mean a carefully considered resolution to do or not to do something. But actions, and accidents, and speeches will be considered with reference to three different times; what a man has done, what has happened to him, or what he has said; or what he is doing, or what is happening to him, or what he is saying; or what he is going to do, what is about to happen to him, or what speech he is about to deliver. And all these things appear to be attributable to persons.

XXVI. But of the considerations which belong to things, some are connected with the thing itself which is the subject of discussion; some are considered in the performance of the thing; some are united with the thing itself; some follow in the accomplishment of the thing. Those things are connected with the thing itself which appear always to be attached to the thing and which cannot be separated from it. The first of such things is a brief exposition of the whole business, which contains the sum of the entire matter, in this way—"The slaying of a parent;" "the betrayal of a country." Then comes the cause of this general fact; and we inquire by what means, and in what manner, and with what view such and such a thing has been done. After that we inquire what was done before this action under consideration was done, and all the steps which preceded this action. After that, what was done in the very execution of this action. And last of all, what has been done since.

But with reference to the performance of an action, which was the second topic of those which were attributed to things, the place, and the time, and the manner, and the opportunity, and the facilities will be inquired into. The place is taken into consideration in which the thing was done; with reference to the opportunity which the doer seems to have had of executing the business; and that opportunity is measured by the importance of the action, by the interval which has elapsed, by the distance, by the nearness, by the solitude of the place, or by the frequented character of it, by the nature of the spot itself and by the neighbourhood of the whole region. And it is estimated also with reference to these characteristics, whether the place be sacred or not, public or private, whether it belongs or has belonged to some one else, or to the man whose conduct is under consideration.

But the time is, that, I mean, which we are speaking of at the present moment, (for it is difficult to define it in a general view of it with any exactness,) a certain portion of eternity with some fixed limitation of annual or monthly, or daily or nightly space. In reference to this we take into consideration the things which are passed, and those things which, by reason of the time which has elapsed since, have become so obsolete as to be considered incredible, and to be already classed among the number of fables, and those things also which, having been performed a long time ago and at a time remote from our recollection, still affect us with a belief that they have been handed down truly, because certain memorials of those facts are extant in written documents, and those things which have been done lately, so that most people are able to be acquainted with them. And also those things which exist at the present moment, and which are actually taking place now, and which are the consequences of former actions. And with reference to those things it is open to us to consider which will happen sooner, and which later. And also generally in considering questions of time, the distance or proximity of the time is to be taken into account: for it is often proper to measure the business done with the time occupied in doing it, and to consider whether a business of such and such magnitude, or whether such and such a multitude of things, can be performed in that time. And we should take into consideration the time of year, and of the month, and of the day, and of the night, and the watches, and the hours, and each separate portion of any one of these times.

XXVII. An occasion is a portion of time having in it a suitable opportunity for doing or avoiding to do some particular thing. Wherefore there is this difference between it and time. For, as to genus, indeed, they are both understood to be identical; but in time some space is expressed in some manner or other, which is regarded with reference to years, or to a year, or to some portion of a year, but in an occasion, besides the space of time implied in the word, there is indicated an especial opportunity of doing something. As therefore the two are identical in genus it is some portion and species as it were, in which the one differs, as we have said, from the other.

Now occasion is distributed into three classes, public, common and singular. That is a public occasion, which the whole city avails itself of for some particular cause, as games, a day of festival, or war. That is a common occasion which happens to all men at nearly the same time, as the harvest, the vintage, summer, or winter. That is a singular occasion, which, on account of some special cause, happens at times to some private individuals, as for instance, a wedding, a sacrifice, a funeral, a feast, sleep.

But the manner, also, is inquired into, in what manner, how, and with what design the action was done? Its parts are, the doer knowing what he was about, and not knowing. But the degree of his knowledge is measured by these circumstances whether the doer did his action secretly, openly, under compulsion or through persuasion. The fact of the absence of knowledge is brought forward as an excuse, and its parts are actual ignorance, accident, necessity. It is also attributed to agitation of mind, that is, to annoyance, to passion to love, and to other feelings of a similar class. Facilities, are those circumstances owing to which a thing is done more easily, or without which a thing cannot be done at all.

XXVIII. And it is understood that there is added to the general consideration of the whole matter, the consideration what is greater than and what is less than, and what is like the affair which is under discussion, and what is equally important with it, and what is contrary to it, and what is negatively opposed to it, and the whole classification of the affair, and the divisions of it, and the ultimate result. The cases of greater, and less and equally important, are considered with reference to the power, and number and form of the business, as if we were regarding the stature of a human body.

Now what is similar arises out of a species admitting of comparisons. Now what admits of comparisons is estimated by a nature which may be compared with it, and likened to it. What is contrary, is what is placed in a different class and is as distant as possible from that thing to which it is called contrary, as cold is from heat and death from life. But that is negatively opposed to a thing which is separated from the thing by an opposition which is limited to a denial of the quality; in this way, "to be wise," and "not to be wise." That is a genus which embraces several species, as "Cupidity." That is a species which is subordinate to a genus, as "Love," "Avarice." The Result is the ultimate termination of any business; in which it is a common inquiry, what has resulted from each separate fact; what is resulting from it; what is likely to result from it. Wherefore, in order that that which is likely to happen may be more conveniently comprehended in the mind with respect to this genus, we ought first to consider what is accustomed to result from every separate circumstance; in this manner:—From arrogance, hatred usually results; and from insolence, arrogance.

The fourth division is a natural consequence from those qualities, which we said were usually attributed to things in distinction from persons. And with respect to this, those circumstances are sought for which ensue from a thing being done. In the first place, by what name it is proper that that which has been done should be called. In the next place, who have been the chief agents in, or originators of that action; and last of all, who have been the approvers and the imitators of that precedent and of that discovery. In the next place, whether there is any regular usage established with regard to that case, or whether there is any regular rule bearing on that case, or any regular course of proceeding, any formal decision, any science reduced to rules, any artificial system. In the next place, whether its nature is in the habit of being ordinarily displayed, or whether it is so very rarely, and whether it is quite unaccustomed to be so. After that, whether men are accustomed to approve of such a case with their authority, or to be offended at such actions; and with what eyes they look upon the other circumstances which are in the habit of following any similar conduct, either immediately or after an interval. And in the very last place, we must take notice whether any of those circumstances which are rightly classed under honesty or utility ensue. But as to these matters it will be necessary to speak more clearly when we come to mention the deliberative kind of argument. And the circumstances which we have now mentioned are those which are usually attributed to things as opposed to persons.

XXIX. But all argumentation, which can be derived from those topics which we have mentioned, ought to be either probable or unavoidable. Indeed, to define it in a few words, argumentation appears to be an invention of some sort, which either shows something or other in a probable manner, or demonstrates it in an irrefutable one. Those things are demonstrated irrefutably which can neither be done nor proved in any other manner whatever than that in which they are stated; in this manner:—"If she has had a child, she has lain with a man." This sort of arguing, which is conversant with irrefutable demonstration, is especially used in speaking in the way of dilemma, or enumeration, or simple inference.

Dilemma is a case in which, whichever admission you make, you are found fault with. For example:—"If he is a worthless fellow, why are you intimate with him? If he is an excellent man, why do you accuse him?" Enumeration is a statement in which, when many matters have been stated and all other arguments invalidated, the one which remains is inevitably proved; in this manner:—"It is quite plain that he was slain by this man, either because of his enmity to him, or some fear, or hope, which he had conceived, or in order to gratify some friend of his; or, if none of these alternatives are true, then that he was not slain by him at all; for a great crime cannot be undertaken without a motive. But he had no quarrel with him, nor fear of him, nor hope of any advantage to be gained by his death, nor did his death in the least concern any friend of his. It remains, therefore, that he was not slain by him at all." But a simple inference is declared from a necessary consequence, in this way:—"If you say that I did that at that time, at that time I was beyond the sea; it follows, that I not only did not do what you say I did, but that it was not even possible for me to have done it." And it will be desirable to look to this very carefully, in order that this sort of inference may not be refuted in any manner, so that the proof may not only have some sort of argument in it, and some resemblance to an unavoidable conclusion, but that the very argument itself may proceed on irrefutable reasons.

But that is probable which is accustomed generally to take place, or which depends upon the opinion of men, or which contains some resemblance to these properties, whether it be false or true. In that description of subject the most usual probable argument is something of this sort:—"If she is his mother, she loves her son." "If he is an avaricious man, he neglects his oath." But in the case which depends mainly on opinion, probable arguments are such as this: "That there are punishments prepared in the shades below for impious men."—"That those men who give their attention to philosophy do not think that there are gods."

XXX. But resemblance is chiefly seen in things which are contrary to one another, or equal to one another, and in those things which fall under the same principle. In things contrary to one another, in this manner:—"For if it is right that those men should be pardoned who have injured me unintentionally, it is also fitting that one should feel no gratitude towards those who have benefited me because they could not help it."

In things equal to one another, in this way:—"For as a place without a harbour cannot be safe for ships, so a mind without integrity cannot be trustworthy for a man's friends." In those things which fall under the same principle a probable argument is considered in this way:—"For if it be not discreditable to the Rhodians to let out their port dues, then it is not discreditable even to Hermacreon to rent them." Then these arguments are true, in this manner:—"Since there is a scar, there has been a wound." Then they are probable, in in this way:—"If there was a great deal of dust on his shoes, he must have come off a journey." But (in order that we may arrange this matter in certain definite divisions) every probable argument which is assumed for the purpose of discussion, is either a proof, or something credible, or something already determined; or something which may be compared with something else.

That is a proof which falls under some particular sense, and which indicates something which appears to have proceeded from it, which either existed previously, or was in the thing itself, or has ensued since, and, nevertheless, requires the evidence of testimony, and a more authoritative confirmation,—as blood, flight, dust, paleness, and other tokens like these. That is a credible statement which, without any witness being heard, is confirmed in the opinion of the hearer; in this way:—There is no one who does not wish his children to be free from injury, and happy. A case decided beforehand, is a matter approved of by the assent, or authority, or judgment of some person or persons. It is seen in three kinds of decision;—the religious one, the common one, the one depending on sanction. That is a religious one, which men on their oaths have decided in accordance with the laws. That is a common one, which all men have almost in a body approved of and adopted; in this manner:—"That all men should rise up on the appearance of their elders; That all men should pity suppliants." That depends on sanction, which, as it was a doubtful point what ought to be considered its character, men have established of their own authority; as, for instance, the conduct of the father of Gracchus, whom the Roman people made consul after his censorship, because he had done nothing in his censorship without the knowledge of his colleague.

But that is a decision admitting of comparisons, which in a multitude of different circumstances contains some principle which is alike in all. Its parts are three,—

representation, collation, example. A Representation is a statement demonstrating some resemblance of bodies or natures; Collation is a statement comparing one thing with another, because of their likeness to one another; Example is that which confirms or invalidates a case by some authority, or by what has happened to some man, or under some especial circumstances. Instances of these things, and descriptions of them, will be given amid the precepts for oratory. And the source of all confirmations has been already explained as occasion offered, and has been demonstrated no less clearly than the nature of the case required. But how each separate statement, and each part of a statement, and every dispute ought to be handled,—whether we refer to verbal discussion or to writings,—and what arguments are suitable for each kind of discussion, we will mention, speaking separately of each kind, in the second book. At present we have only dropped hints about the numbers, and moods, and parts of arguing in an irregular and promiscuous manner; hereafter we will digest (making careful distinctions between and selections from each kind of cause) what is suitable for each kind of discussion, culling it out of this abundance which we have already displayed.

And indeed every sort of argument can be discovered from among these topics; and that, when discovered, it should be embellished, and separated in certain divisions, is very agreeable, and highly necessary, and is also a thing which has been greatly neglected by writers on this art. Wherefore at this present time it is desirable for us to speak of that sort of instruction, in order that perfection of arguing may be added to the discovery of proper arguments. And all this topic requires to be considered with great care and diligence, because there is not only great usefulness in this matter, but there is also extreme difficulty in giving precepts.

XXXI. All argumentation, therefore, is to be carried on either by induction, or by ratiocination. Induction is a manner of speaking which, by means of facts which are not doubtful, forces the assent of the person to whom it is addressed. By which assent it causes him even to approve of some points which are doubtful, on account of their resemblance to those things to which he has assented; as in the Æschines of Socrates, Socrates shows that Aspasia used to argue with Xenophon's wife, and with Xenophon himself. "Tell me, I beg of you, O you wife of Xenophon, if your neighbour has better gold than you have, whether you prefer her gold or your own?" "Hers," says she. "Suppose she has dresses and other ornaments suited to women, of more value than those which you have, should you prefer your own or hers?" "Hers, to be sure," answered she. "Come, then," says Aspasia, "suppose she has a better husband than you have, should you then prefer your own husband or hers?" On this the woman blushed.

But Aspasia began a discourse with Xenophon himself. "I ask you, O Xenophon," says she, "if your neighbour has a better horse than yours is, whether you would prefer your own horse or his?" "His," says he. "Suppose he has a better farm than you have, which farm, I should like to know, would you prefer to possess?" "Beyond all doubt," says he, "that which is the best." "Suppose he has a better wife than you have, would you prefer his wife?" And on this Xenophon himself was silent. Then spake Aspasia,—"Since each of you avoids answering me that question alone which was the only one which I wished to have answered, I will tell you what each of you are thinking of; for both you, O woman, wish to have the best husband, and you, O Xenophon, most exceedingly desire to have the most excellent wife. Wherefore, unless you both so contrive matters that there shall not be on the whole earth a more excellent man or a more admirable woman, then in truth you will at all times desire above all things that which you think to be the best thing in the world, namely, that you, O Xenophon, may be the husband of the best possible wife; and you, O woman, that you may be married to the most excellent husband possible." After they had declared their assent to these far from doubtful propositions, it followed, on account of the resemblance of the cases, that if any one had separately asked them about some doubtful point, that also would have been admitted as certain, on account of the method employed in putting the question.

This was a method of instruction which Socrates used to a great extent, because he himself preferred bringing forward no arguments for the purpose of persuasion, but wished rather that the person with whom he was disputing should form his own conclusions from arguments with which he had furnished himself, and which he was unavoidably compelled to approve of from the grounds which he had already assented to.

XXXII. And with reference to this kind of persuasion, it appears to me desirable to lay down a rule, in the first place, that the argument which we bring forward by way of simile, should be such that it is impossible to avoid admitting it. For the premiss on account of which we intend to demand that that point which is doubtful shall be conceded to us, ought not to be doubtful itself. In the next place, we must take care that that point, for the sake of establishing which the induction is made, shall be really like those things which we have adduced before as matters admitting of no question. For it will be of no service to us that something has been already admitted, if that for the sake of which we were desirous to get that statement admitted be unlike it; so that the hearer may not understand what is the use of those original inductions, or to what result they tend.

For the man who sees that, if he is correct in giving his assent to the thing about which he is first asked, that thing also to which he does not agree must unavoidably be admitted by him, very often will not allow the examination to proceed any further, either by not answering at all, or by answering wrongly. Wherefore it is necessary that he should, by the method in which the inquiry is conducted, be led on without perceiving it, from the admissions which he has already made, to admit that which he is not inclined to admit, and at last he must either decline to give an answer, or he must admit what is wanted, or he must deny it. If the proposition be denied, then we must either show its resemblance to those things which have been already admitted or we must employ some other induction. If it be granted, then the argumentation may be brought to a close. If he keeps silence, then an answer must be extracted, or, since silence is very like a confession, it may be as well to bring the discussion to a close, taking the silence to be equivalent to an admission.

And so this kind of argumentation is threefold. The first part consists of one simile, or of several, the second, of that which we desire to have admitted, for the sake of which the similes have been employed, the third proceeds from the conclusion which either establishes the admissions which have been made or points out what may be established from it.

XXXIII. But because it will not appear to some people to have been explained with sufficient clearness, unless we submit some instance taken from the civil class of causes, it seems desirable to employ some example of this sort, not because the rules to be laid down differ, or because it is expedient to employ such differently in this sort of discussion from what we should in ordinary discourse, but in order to satisfy the desire of those men, who, though they may have seen something in one place, are unable to recognise it in another unless it be proved. Therefore in this cause which is very notorious among the Greeks, that of Epaminondas, the general of the Thebans, who did not give up his army to the magistrate who succeeded him in due course of law, and when he himself had retained his army a few days contrary to law, he utterly defeated the

Lacedaemonians, the accuser might employ an argumentation by means of induction, while defending the letter of the law in opposition to its spirit, in this way:—

"If, O judges, the framer of the law had added to his law what Epaminondas says that he intended, and had subjoined the exception 'except where any one has omitted to deliver up his army for the advantage of the republic,' would you have endured it? I think not. And if you yourselves, (though, such a proceeding is very far from your religious habits and from your wisdom,) for the sake of doing honour to this man, were to order the same exception to be subjoined to the law, would the Theban people endure that such a thing should be done? Beyond all question it would not endure it. Can it possibly then appear to you that that which would be scandalous if it were added to a law, should be proper to be done just as if it had been added to the law? I know your acuteness well; it cannot seem so to you, O judges. But if the intention of the framer of the law cannot be altered as to its expressions either by him or by you, then beware lest it should be a much more scandalous thing that that should be altered in fact, and by your decision, which cannot be altered in one single word."

And we seem now to have said enough for the present respecting induction. Next, let us consider the power and nature of ratiocination.

XXXIV. Ratiocination is a sort of speaking, eliciting something probable from the fact under consideration itself, which being explained and known of itself, confirms itself by its own power and principles.

Those who have thought it profitable to pay diligent attention to this kind of reasoning, have differed a little in the manner in which they have laid down rules, though they were aiming at the same end as far as the practice of speaking went. For some of them have said that there are five divisions of it, and some have thought that it had no more parts than could be arranged under three divisions. And it would seem not useless to explain the dispute which exists between these parties, with the reasons which each allege for it; for it is a short one, and not such that either party appears to be talking nonsense. And this topic also appears to us to be one that it is not at all right to omit in speaking.

Those who think that it ought to be arranged in five divisions, say that first of all it is desirable to explain the sum of the discussion, in this way:—Those things are better managed which are done on some deliberate plan, than those which are conducted without any steady design. This they call the first division. And then they think it right that it should be further proved by various arguments, and by as copious statements as possible; in this way:—"That house which is governed by reason is better appointed in all things, and more completely furnished, than that which is conducted at random, and on no settled plan;—that army which is commanded by a wise and skilful general, is governed more suitably in all particulars than that which is managed by the folly and rashness of any one. The same principle prevails with respect to sailing; for that ship performs its voyage best which has the most experienced pilot."

When the proposition has been proved in this manner, and when two parts of the ratiocination have proceeded, they say in the third part, that it is desirable to assume, from the mere intrinsic force of the proposition, what you wish to prove; in this way:— "But none of all those things is managed better than the entire world." In the fourth division they adduce besides another argument in proof of this assumption, in this manner:—"For both the rising and setting of the stars preserve some definite order, and their annual commutations do not only always take place in the same manner by some express necessity, but they are also adapted to the service of everything, and their daily and nightly changes have never injured anything in any particular from being altered capriciously." And all these things are a token that the nature of the world has been arranged by no ordinary wisdom. In the fifth division they bring forward that sort of statement, which either adduces that sort of fact alone which is compelled in every possible manner, in this way:—"The world, therefore, is governed on some settled plan;" or else, when it has briefly united both the proposition and the assumption, it adds this which is derived from both of them together, in this way:—"But if those things are managed better which are conducted on a settled plan, than those which are conducted without such settled plan; and if nothing whatever is managed better than the entire world; therefore it follows that the world is managed on a settled plan." And in this way they think that such argumentation has five divisions.

XXXV. But those who affirm that it has only three divisions, do not think that the argumentation ought to be conducted in any other way, but they find fault with this arrangement of the divisions. For they say that neither the proposition nor the assumption ought to be separated from their proofs; and that a proposition does not appear to be complete, nor an assumption perfect, which is not corroborated by proof. Therefore, they say that what those other men divide into two parts, proposition and proof, appears to them one part only, namely proposition. For if it be not proved, the proposition has no business to make part of the argumentation. In the same way they say that that which those other men call the assumption, and the proof of the assumption, appears to them to be assumption only. And the result is, that the whole argumentation being treated in the same way, appears to some susceptible of five divisions, and to others of only three; so that the difference does not so much affect the practice of speaking, as the principles on which the rules are to be laid down.

But to us that arrangement appears to be more convenient which divides it under five heads; and that is the one which all those who come from the school of Aristotle, or of Theophrastus, have chiefly followed. For as it is chiefly Socrates and the disciples of Socrates who have employed that former sort of argumentation which goes on induction, so this which is wrought up by ratiocination has been exceedingly practised by Aristotle, and the Peripatetics, and Theophrastus; and after them by those rhetoricians who are accounted the most elegant and the most skilful. And it seems desirable to explain why that arrangement is more approved of by us, that we may not appear to have adopted it capriciously; at the same time we must be brief in the explanation, that we may not appear to dwell on such subjects longer than the general manner of laying down rules requires.

XXXVI. If in any sort of argumentation it is sufficient to use a proposition by itself, and if it is not requisite to add proof to the proposition; but if in any sort of argumentation a proposition is of no power unless proof be added to it; then proof is something distinct from the proposition. For that which can be joined to a thing or separated from it, cannot possibly be the same thing with that to which it is joined or from which it is separated. But there is a certain kind of argumentation in which the proposition does not require confirmatory proof, and also another kind in which it is of no use at all without such proof, as we shall show. Proof, then, is a thing different from a proposition. And we will demonstrate that point which we have promised to show in this way:—The proposition which contains in itself something manifest, because it is unavoidable that that should be admitted by all men, has no necessity for our desiring to prove and corroborate it.

It is a sort of statement like this:—"If on the day on which that murder was committed at Rome, I was at Athens, I could not have been present at that murder." Because this is manifestly true, there is no need to adduce proof of it; wherefore, it is proper at once to assume the fact, in this way:—"But I was at Athens on that day." If this is not notorious, it requires proof; and when the proof is furnished the conclusion must follow:—"Therefore I could not have been present at the murder." There is, therefore, a certain kind of proposition which does not require proof. For why need one waste time in proving that there is a kind which does require proof; for that is easily visible to all men. And if this be the case, from this fact, and from that statement which we have established, it follows that proof is something distinct from a proposition. And if it is so, it is evidently false that argumentation is susceptible of only three divisions.

In the same manner it is plain that there is another sort of proof also which is distinct from assumption. For if in some sort of argumentation it is sufficient to use assumption, and if it is not requisite to add proof to the assumption; and if, again, in some sort of argumentation assumption is invalid unless proof be added to it; then proof is something separate and distinct from assumption. But there is a kind of argumentation in which assumption does not require proof; and a certain other kind in which it is of no use without proof; as we shall show. Proof, then, is a thing distinct from assumption. And we will demonstrate that which we have promised to in this manner.

That assumption which contains a truth evident to all men has no need of proof. That is an assumption of this sort:—"If it be desirable to be wise, it is proper to pay attention to philosophy." This proposition requires proof. For it is not self-evident. Nor is it notorious to all men, because many think that philosophy is of no service at all, and some think that it is even a disservice. A self-evident assumption is such as this:—"But it is desirable to be wise." And because this is of itself evident from the simple fact, and is at once perceived to be true, there is no need that it be proved. Wherefore, the argumentation may be at once terminated:—"Therefore it is proper to pay attention to philosophy." There is, therefore, a certain kind of assumption which does not stand in need of proof; for it is evident that is a kind which does. Therefore, it is false that argumentation is susceptible of only a threefold division.

XXXVII. And from these considerations that also is evident, that there is a certain kind of argumentation in which neither proposition nor assumption stands in need of proof, of this sort, that we may adduce something undoubted and concise, for the sake of example. "If wisdom is above all things to be desired, then folly is above all things to be avoided; but wisdom is to be desired above all things, therefore folly is above all things to be avoided." Here both the assumption and the proposition are self-evident, on which account neither of them stands in need of proof. And from all these facts it is manifest that proof is at times added, and at times is not added. From which it is palpable that proof is not contained in a proposition, nor in an assumption, but that each being placed in its proper place, has its own peculiar force fixed and belonging to itself. And if that is the case, then those men have made a convenient arrangement who have divided argumentation into five parts.

Are there five parts of that argumentation which is carried on by ratiocination? First of all, proposition, by which that topic is briefly explained from which all the force of the ratiocination ought to proceed. Then the proof of the proposition, by which that which has been briefly set forth being corroborated by reasons, is made more probable and evident. Then assumption, by which that is assumed which, proceeding from the proposition, has its effect on proving the case. Then the proof of the assumption, by which that which has been assumed is confirmed by reasons. Lastly, the summing up, in which that which results from the entire argumentation is briefly explained. So the argumentation which has the greatest number of divisions consists of these five parts.

The second sort of argumentation has four divisions; the third has three. Then there is one which has two; which, however, is a disputed point. And about each separate division it is possible that some people may think that there is room for a discussion.

XXXVIII. Let us then bring forward some examples of those matters which are agreed upon. And in favour of those which are doubtful, let us bring forward some reasons. Now the argumentation which is divided into five divisions is of this sort:—It is desirable, O judges, to refer all laws to the advantage of the republic, and to interpret them with reference to the general advantage, and according to the strict wording according to which they are drawn up. For our ancestors were men of such virtue and such wisdom, that when they were drawing up laws, they proposed to themselves no other object than the safety and advantage of the republic; for they were neither willing themselves to draw up any law which could be injurious; and if they had drawn up one of such a character, they were sure that it would be rejected when its tendency was perceived. For no one wishes to preserve the laws for the sake of the laws, but for the sake of the republic; because all men believe that the republic is best managed by means of laws. It is desirable, therefore, to interpret all written laws with reference to that cause for the sake of which it is desirable that the laws should be preserved. That is to say, since we are servants of the republic, let us interpret the laws with reference to the advantage and benefit of the republic. For as it is not right to think that anything results from medicine except what has reference to the advantage of the body, since it is for the sake of the body that the science of medicine has been established; so it is desirable to think that nothing proceeds from the laws except what is for the advantage of the republic, since it is for the sake of the republic that laws were instituted.

Therefore, while deciding on this point, cease to inquire about the strict letter of the law, and consider the law (as it is reasonable to do) with reference to the advantage of the republic. For what was more advantageous for the Thebans than for the Lacedaemonians to be put down? What object was Epaminondas, the Theban general, more bound to aim at than the victory of the Thebans? What had he any right to consider more precious or more dear to him, than the great glory then acquired by the Thebans, than such an illustrious and magnificent trophy? Surely, disregarding the letter of the law, it became him to consider the intention of the framer of the law. And this now has been sufficiently insisted on, namely, that no law has ever been drawn up by any one, that had not for its object the benefit of the commonwealth. He then thought that it was the very extremity of madness, not to interpret with reference to the advantage of the republic, that which had been framed for the sake of the safety of the republic. And it is right to interpret all laws with reference to the safety of the republic; and if he was a great instrument of the safety of the republic, certainly it is quite impossible that he by one and the same action should have consulted the general welfare, and yet should have violated the laws.

XXXIX. But argumentation consists of four parts, when we either advance a proposition, or claim an assumption without proof. That it is proper to do when either the proposition is understood by its own merits, or when the assumption is self-evident and is in need of no proof. If we pass over the proof of the proposition, the argumentation then consists of four parts, and is conducted in this manner:—"O judges, you who are deciding on your oaths, in accordance with the law, ought to obey the laws; but you cannot obey the laws unless you follow that which is written in the law. For what more certain evidence of his intention could the framer of a law leave behind him, than that which he himself wrote with great care and diligence? But if there were no written documents, then we should be very anxious for them, in order that the intention of the framer of the law might be ascertained; nor should we permit Epaminondas, not even if he were beyond the power of this tribunal, to interpret to us the meaning of the law; much less will we now permit him, when, the law is at hand, to interpret the intention of the lawgiver, not from that which is most clearly written, but from that which is convenient for his own cause. But if you, O judges, are bound to obey the laws, and if you are unable to do so unless you follow what is written in the law; what can hinder your deciding that he has acted contrary to the laws?"

But if we pass over the proof of the assumption, again the argumentation will be arranged under four heads, in this manner:—"When men have repeatedly deceived us, having pledged their faith to us, we ought not to give credit to anything that they say for if we receive any injury; in consequence of their perfidy, there will be no one except ourselves whom we shall have any right to accuse. And in the first place, it is inconvenient to be deceived, in the next place, it is foolish, thirdly, it is disgraceful. But the Carthaginians have before this deceived us over and over again. It is therefore the greatest insanity to rest any hopes on their good faith, when you have been so often deceived by their treachery."

When the proof both of the proposition and of the assumption is passed over, the argumentation becomes threefold only, in this way—"We must either live in fear of the Carthaginians if we leave them with their power undiminished, or we must destroy their city. And certainly it is not desirable to live in fear of them. The only remaining alternative then is to destroy their city."

XL But some people think that it is both possible and advisable at times to pass over the summing up altogether, when it is quite evident what is effected by ratiocination. And then if that be done they consider that the argumentation is limited to two divisions, in this way—"If she has had a child she is not a virgin. But she has had a child." In this case they say it is quite sufficient to state the proposition and assumption, since it is quite plain that the matter which is here stated is such as does not stand in need of summing up. But to us it seems that all ratiocination ought to be terminated in proper form and that that defect which offends them is above all things to be avoided namely, that of introducing what is self evident into the summing up.

But this will be possible to be effected if we come to a right understanding of the different kinds of summing up. For we shall either sum up in such a way as to unite together the proposition and the assumption, in this way—"But if it is right for all laws to be referred to the general advantage of the republic, and if this man ensured the safety of the republic, undoubtedly he cannot by one and the same action have consulted the general safety and yet have violated the laws,"—or thus, in order that the opinion we advocate may be established by arguments drawn from contraries, in this manner—"It is then the very greatest madness to build hopes on the good faith of those men by whose treachery you have been so repeatedly deceived,"—or so that that inference alone be drawn which is already announced, in this manner—"Let us then destroy their city,"—or so that the conclusion which is desired must necessarily follow from the assertion which has been established, in this way—"If she has had a child, she has laid with a man. But she has had a child." This then is established. "Therefore she has lain with a man." If you are unwilling to draw this inference, and prefer inferring what follows, "Therefore she has committed incest," you will have terminated your argumentation but you will have missed an evident and natural summing up.

Wherefore in long argumentations it is often desirable to draw influences from combinations of circumstances, or from contraries. And briefly to explain that point alone which is established, and in those in which the result is evident, to employ arguments drawn from consequences. But if there are any people who think that argumentation ever consists of one part alone they will be able to say that it is often sufficient to carry-on an argumentation in this way.—"Since she has had a child, she has lain with a man." For they say that this assertion requires no proof, nor assumption, nor proof of an assumption, nor summing up. But it seems to us that they are misled by the ambiguity of the name. For argumentation signifies two things under one name, because any discussion respecting anything which is either probable or necessary is called argumentation, and so also is the systematic polishing of such a discussion.

When then they bring forward any statement of this kind,—"Since she has had a child, she has lain, with a man," they bring forward a plain assertion, not a highly worked up argument, but we are speaking of the parts of a highly worked up argument.

XLI. That principle then has nothing to do with this matter. And with the help of this distinction we will remove other obstacles which seem to be in the way of this classification, if any people think that it is possible that at times the assumption may be omitted, and at other times the proposition, and if this idea has in it anything probable or necessary, it is quite inevitable that it must affect the hearer in some great degree. And if it were the only object in view, and if it made no difference in what manner that argument which had been projected was handled, it would be a great mistake to suppose that there is such a vast difference between the greatest orators and ordinary ones.

But it will be exceedingly desirable to infuse variety into our speech, for in all cases sameness is the mother of satiety. That will be able to be managed if we not always enter upon our argumentation in a similar manner. For in the first place it is desirable to distinguish our orations as to their kinds, that is to say, at one time to employ induction, and at another ratiocination. In the next place, in the argumentation itself, it is best not always to begin with the proposition, nor in every case to employ all the five divisions, nor always to work up the different parts in the same manner, but it is permissible sometimes to begin with the assumption, sometimes with one or other of the proofs, sometimes with both, sometimes to employ one kind of summing up, and sometimes another. And in order that this variety may be seen, let us either write, or in any example whatever let us exercise this same principle with respect to those things which we endeavour to prove, that our task may be as easy as possible.

And concerning the parts of the argumentation it seems to us that enough has been said. But we wish to have it understood that we hold the doctrine that argumentations are handled in philosophy in many other manners, and those too at times obscure ones, concerning which, however, there is still some definite system laid down. But still those methods appear to us to be inconsistent with the practice of an orator. But as to those things which we think belong to orators, we do not indeed undertake to say that we have attended to them more carefully than others have, but we do assert that we have written on them with more accuracy and diligence. At present let us go on in regular order to the other points, as we originally proposed.

XLII. Reprehension is that by means of which the proof adduced by the opposite party is invalidated by arguing, or is disparaged, or is reduced to nothing. And this sort of argument proceeds from the same source of invention which confirmation employs, because whatever the topics may be by means of which any statement can be confirmed, the very same may be used in order to invalidate it. For nothing is to be considered in all these inventions, except that which has been attributed to persons or to things. Wherefore it will be necessary that the invention and the high polish which ought to be given to argumentation must be transferred to this part of our oration also from those rules which have been already laid down. But in order that we may give some precepts with reference to this part also, we will explain the different methods of reprehension, and those who observe them will more easily be able to do away with or invalidate those statements which are made on the opposite side.

All argumentation is reprehended when anything, whether it be one thing only, or more than one of those positions which are assumed, is not granted, or if, though they are granted, it is denied that the conclusion legitimately follows from them, or if it is shown that the very kind of argumentation is faulty, or if in opposition to one form and reliable sort of argumentation another is employed which is equally firm and convincing. Something of those positions which have been assumed is not granted when either that thing which the opposite party says is credible is denied to be such, or when what they think admits of a comparison with the present case is shown to be unlike it, or when what has been already decided is either turned aside as referring to something else, or is impeached as having been erroneously decided, or when that which the opposite party have called a proof is denied to be such, or if the summing up is denied in some one point or in every particular, or if it is shown that the enumeration of matters stated and proved is incorrect, or if the simple conclusion is proved to contain something false. For everything which is assumed for the purpose of arguing on, whether as necessary or as only probable, must inevitably be assumed from these topics, as we have already pointed out.

XLIII. What is assumed as something credible is invalidated, if it is either manifestly false, in this way:—"There is the one who would not prefer riches to wisdom." Or on the opposite side something credible may be brought against it, in this manner—"Who is there who is not more desirous of doing his duty than of acquiring money?" Or it may be utterly and absolutely incredible, as if some one, who it is notorious is a miser, were to say that he had neglected the acquisition of some large sum of money for the sake of performing some inconsiderable duty. Or if that which happens in some circumstances, and to some persons, were asserted to happen habitually in all cases and to everybody, in this way.—'Those men who are poor have a greater regard for money than for duty.' 'It is very natural that a murder should have been committed in that which is a desert place.' How could a man be murdered in a much frequented place? Or if a thing which is done seldom is asserted never to be done at all, as Curius asserts in his speech in behalf of Fulvius, where he says, "No one can fall in love at a single glance, or as he is passing by."

But that which is assumed as a proof may be invalidated by a recurrence to the same topics as those by which it is sought to be established. For in a proof the first thing to be shown is that it is true, and in the next place, that it is one especially affecting the matter which is under discussion, as blood is a proof of murder in the next place, that that has been done which ought not to have been, or that has not been done which ought to have been and last of all, that the person accused was acquainted with the law and usages affecting the matter which is the subject of inquiry. For all these circumstance are matters requiring proof, and we will explain them more carefully, when we come to speak about conjectural statements separately. Therefore, each of these points in a reprehension of the statement of the adversary must be laboured, and it must be shown either that such and such a thing is no proof, or that it is an unimportant proof, or that it is favourable to oneself rather than to the adversary, or that it is altogether erroneously alleged, or that it may be diverted so as to give grounds to an entirely different suspicion.

XLIV. But when anything is alleged as a proper object of comparison, since that is a class of argument which turns principally on resemblance, in reprehending the adversity it will be advisable to deny that there is any resemblance at all to the case with which it is attempted to institute the comparison. And that may be done if it be proved to be different in genus or in nature, or in power, or in magnitude, or in time or place, or with reference to the person affected, or to the opinions generally entertained of it. And if it be shown also in what classification that which is brought forward on account of the alleged resemblance and in what place too the whole genus with reference to which it is brought forward, ought to be placed. After that it will be pointed out how the one thing differs from the other, from which we shall proceed to show that a different opinion ought to be entertained of that which is brought forward by way of comparison, and of that to which it is sought to be compared. And this sort of argument we especially require when that particular argumentation which is carried on by means of induction is to be reprehended. If any previous decision be alleged, since these are the topics by which it is principally established, the praise of those who have delivered such decision, the resemblance of the matter which is at present under discussion to that which has already been the subject of the decision referred to, that not only the decision is not found fault with because it is mentioned, but that it is approved of by every one, and by showing too, that the case which has been already decided is a more difficult and a more important one than that which is under consideration now. It will be desirable also to invalidate it by arguments drawn from the contrary topics, if either truth or probability will allow us to do so. And it will be necessary to take care and notice whether the matter which has been decided has any real connexion with that which is the present subject of discussion, and we must also take care that no case is adduced in which any error has been committed, so that it should seem that we are passing judgment on the man himself who has delivered the decision referred to.

It is desirable further to take care that they do not bring forward some solitary or unusual decision when there have been many decisions given the other way. For by such means as this the authority of the decision alleged can be best invalidated. And it is desirable that those arguments which are assumed as probable should be handled in this way.

XLV. But those which are brought forward as necessary, if they are only imitations of a necessary kind of argumentation and are not so in reality, may be reprehended in this manner. In the first place, the summing up, which ought to take away the force of the admissions you have made if it be a correct one, will never be reprehended, if it be an incorrect one it may be attacked by two methods, either by conversion or by the invalidating one portion of it. By conversion, in this way:—

> "For if the man be modest, why should you
> Attack so good a man? And if his heart
> And face be seats of shameless impudence,
> Then what avails your accusation
> Of one who views all fame with careless eye?"

In this case, whether you say that he is a modest man or that he is not, he thinks that the unavoidable inference is that you should not accuse him. But that may be reprehended by conversion thus—"But indeed, he ought to be accused, for if he be modest, accuse him, for he will not treat your imputations against him lightly, but if he has a shameless disposition of mind, still accuse him, for in that case he is not a respectable man."

And again, the argument may be reprehended by an invalidating of the other part of it—"But if he is a modest man, when he has been corrected by your accusation he will abandon his error." An enumeration of particulars is understood to be faulty if we either say that something has been passed over which we are willing to admit, or if some weak point has been included in it which can be contradicted, or if there is no reason why we may not honestly admit it. Something is passed over in such an enumeration as this.— "Since you have that horse, you must either have bought it, or have acquired it by inheritance, or have received it as a gift, or he must have been born on your estate, or, if none of these alternatives of the case, you must have stolen it. But you did not buy it, nor did it come to you by inheritance, nor was it foaled on your estate, nor was it given to you as a present, therefore you must certainly have stolen it."

This enumeration is fairly reprehended, if it can be alleged that the horse was taken from the enemy, as that description of booty is not sold. And if that be alleged, the enumeration is disproved, since that matter has been stated which was passed over in such enumeration.

XLVI. But it will also be reprehended in another manner, if any contradictory statement is advanced; that is to say, just by way of example, if, to continue arguing from the previous case, it can be shown that the horse did come to one by inheritance, or if it should not be discreditable to admit the last alternative, as if a person, when his adversaries said,—"You were either laying an ambush against the owner, or you were influenced by a friend, or you were carried away by covetousness," were to confess that he was complying with the entreaties of his friend.

But a simple conclusion is reprehended if that which follows does not appear of necessity to cohere with that which has gone before. For this very proposition, "If he breathes, he is alive," "If it is day, it is light," is a proposition of such a nature that the latter statement appears of necessity to cohere with the preceding one. But this inference, "If she is his mother, she loves him," "If he has ever done wrong, he will never be chastised," ought to be reprehended in such a manner as to show that the latter proposition does not of necessity cohere with the former.

Inferences of this kind, and all other unavoidable conclusions, and indeed all argumentation whatever, and its reprehension too, contains some greater power and has a more extensive operation than is here explained. But the knowledge of this system is such that it cannot be added to any portion of this art, not that it does of itself separately stand in need of a long time, and of deep and arduous consideration. Wherefore those things shall be explained by us at another time, and when we are dealing with another subject, if opportunity be afforded us. At present we ought to be contented with these precepts of the rhetoricians given for the use of orators. When, therefore, any one of these points which are assumed is not granted, the whole statement is invalidated by these means.

XLVII. But when, though these things are admitted, a conclusion is not derived from them, we must consider these points too, whether any other conclusion is obtained, or whether anything else is meant, in this way,—If, when any one says that he is gone to the army, and any one chooses to use this mode of arguing against him, "If you had come to the army you would have been seen by the military tribunes, but you were not seen by them, therefore you did not go to the army." On this case, when you have admitted the proposition, and the assumption, you have got to invalidate the conclusion, for some other inference has been drawn, and not the one which was inevitable.

And at present, indeed, in order that the case might be more easily understood, we have brought forward an example pregnant with a manifest and an enormous error; but it often happens that an error when stated obscurely is taken for a truth; when either you do not recollect exactly what admissions you have made, or perhaps you have granted something as certain which is extremely doubtful. If you have granted something which is doubtful on that side of the question which you yourself understand, then if the adversary should wish to adapt that part to the other part by means of inference, it will be desirable to show, not from the admission which you have made, but from what he has assumed, that an inference is really established; in this manner:—"If you are in need of money, you have not got money. If you have not got money, you are poor. But you are in need of money, for if it were not so you would not pay attention to commerce; therefore you are poor." This is refuted in this way:—"When you said, if you are in need of money you have not got money, I understood you to mean, 'If you are in need of money from poverty, then you have not got money;' and therefore I admitted the argument. But when you assumed, 'But you are in need of money,' I understood you to mean, 'But you wish to have more money.' But from these admissions this result, 'Therefore you are poor,' does not follow. But it would follow if I had made this admission to you in the first instance, that any one who wished to have more money, had no money at all."

XLVIII. But many often think that you have forgotten what admissions you made, and therefore an inference which does not follow legitimately is introduced into the summing up as if it did follow; in this way:—"If the inheritance came to him, it is probable that he was murdered by him." Then they prove this at considerable length. Afterwards they assume, But the inheritance did come to him. Then the inference is deduced; Therefore he did murder him. But that does not necessarily follow from what they had assumed. Wherefore it is necessary to take great care to notice both what is assumed, and what necessarily follows from those assumptions. But the whole description of argumentation will be proved to be faulty on these accounts; if either there is any defect in the argumentation itself, or if it is not adapted to the original intention. And there will be a defect in the argumentation itself, if the whole of it is entirely false, or common, or ordinary, or trifling, or made up of remote suppositions; if the definition contained in it be faulty, if it be controverted, if it be too evident, if it be one which is not admitted, or discreditable, or objected to, or contrary, or inconstant, or adverse to one's object.

That is false in which there is evidently a lie; in this manner:—"That man cannot be wise who neglects money. But Socrates neglected money; therefore he was not wise." That is common which does not make more in favour of our adversaries than of ourselves; in this manner:—"Therefore, O judges, I have summed up in a few words, because I had truth on my side." That is ordinary which, if the admission be now made, can be transferred also to some other case which is not easily proved; in this manner:—"If he had not truth on his side, O judges, he would never have risked committing himself to your decision." That is trifling which is either uttered after the proposition, in this way:—"If it had occurred to him, he would not have done so;" or if a man wishes to conceal a matter manifestly disgraceful under a trifling defence, in this manner:—

"Then when all sought your favour, when your hand
Wielded a mighty sceptre, I forsook you;
But now when all fly from you, I prepare
Alone, despising danger, to restore you."

XLIX. That is remote which is sought to a superfluous extent, in this manner:—"But if Publius Scipio had not given his daughter Cornelia in marriage to Tiberius Gracchus, and if he had not had the two Gracchi by her, such terrible seditions would never have arisen. So that all this distress appears attributable to Scipio." And like this is that celebrated complaint—

> "Oh that the woodman's axe had spared the pine
> That long on Pelion's lofty summit grew." [2]

[2] This is very frequently quoted by Cicero; the Latin lines being the opening of the Medea of Ennius, translated from the first lines of the Medea of Euripides.

For the cause is sought further back than is at all necessary. That is a bad definition, when it either describes common things in this manner:—"He is seditious who is a bad and useless citizen;" for this does not describe the character of a seditious man more than of an ambitious one,—of a calumniator, than of any wicked man whatever, in short. Or when it says anything which is false; in this manner:—"Wisdom is a knowledge how to acquire money." Or when it contains something which is neither dignified nor important; in this way:—"Folly is a desire of inordinate glory." That, indeed, is one folly; but this is defining folly by a species, not by its whole genus. It is controvertible when a doubtful cause is alleged, for the sake of proving a doubtful point; in this manner:—

> "See how the gods who rule the realms above
> And shades below, and all their motions sway,
> Themselves are all in tranquil concord found."

That is self-evident, about which there is no dispute at all. As if any one while accusing Orestes were to make it quite plain that his mother had been put to death by him. That is a disputable definition, when the very thing which we are amplifying is a matter in dispute. As if any one, while accusing Ulysses, were to dwell on this point particularly, that it is a scandalous thing that the bravest of men, Ajax, should have been slain by a most inactive man. That is discreditable which either with respect to the place in which it is spoken, or to the man who utters it, or to the time at which it is uttered, or to those who hear it, or to the matter which is the subject of discussion, appears scandalous on account of the subject being a discreditable one. That is an offensive one, which offends the inclinations of those who hear it; as if any one were to praise the judiciary law of Caepio before the Roman knights, who are themselves desirous of acting as judges.

L. That is a contrary definition, which is laid down in opposition to the actions which those who are the hearers of the speech have done; as if any one were to be speaking before Alexander the Great against some stormer of a city, and were to say that nothing was more inhuman than to destroy cities, when Alexander himself had destroyed Thebes. That is an inconsistent one, which is asserted by the same man in different senses concerning the same case; as if any one, after he has said that the man who has virtue is in need of nothing whatever for the purpose of living well, were afterwards to deny that any one could live well without good health; or that he would stand by a friend in difficulty out of good-will towards him, for that then he would hope that some good would accrue to himself by so doing.

That is an adverse definition, which in some particular is an actual injury to one's own cause; as if any one were to extol the power, and resources, and prosperity of the enemy, while encouraging his own soldiers to fight. If some part of the argumentation is not adapted to the object which is or ought to be proposed to one, it will be found to be owing to some one of these defects. If a man has promised a great many points and proved only a few; or if, when he is bound to prove the whole, he speaks only of some portion; in this way:—The race of women is avaricious; for Eriphyle sold the life of her husband for gold. Or if he does not speak in defence of that particular point which is urged in accusation; as if any one when accused of corruption were to defend himself by the statement that he was brave; as Amphion does in Euripides, and so too in Pacuvius, who, when his musical knowledge is found fault with, praises his knowledge of philosophy. Or if a part of conduct be found fault with on account of the bad character of the man; as if any one were to blame learning on account of the vices of some learned men. Or if any one while wishing to praise somebody were to speak of his good fortune, and not of his virtue; or if any one were to compare one thing with another in such a manner as to think that he was not praising the one unless he was blaming the other; or if he were to praise the one in such a manner as to omit all mention of the other.

Or if, when an inquiry is being carried on respecting one particular point, the speech is addressed to common topics; as if any one, while men are deliberating whether war shall be waged or not, were to devote himself wholly to the praises of peace, and not to proving that that particular war is inexpedient. Or if a false reason for anything be alleged, in this way:—Money is good because it is the thing which, above all others, makes life happy. Or if one is alleged which is invalid, as Plautus says:—

> "Sure to reprove a friend for evident faults
> Is but a thankless office; still 'tis useful,
> And wholesome for a youth of such an age,
> And so this day I will reprove my friend,
> Whose fault is palpable."—*Plautus, Frinummus*, Act i. sc. 2, l.1.

Or in this manner, if a man were to say, "Avarice is the greatest evil; for the desire of money causes great distress to numbers of people." Or it is unsuitable, in this manner:—"Friendship is the greatest good for there are many pleasures in friendship."

LI. The fourth manner of reprehension was stated to be that by which, in opposition to a solid argumentation, one equally, or still more solid, has been advanced. And this kind of argumentation is especially employed in deliberations when we admit that something which is said in opposition to us is reasonable, but still prove that that conduct which we are defending is necessary; or when we confess that the line of conduct which they are advocating is useful, and prove that what we ourselves are contending for is honourable. And we have thought it necessary to say thus much about reprehension; now we will lay down some rules respecting the conclusion.

Hermagoras places digression next in order, and then the ultimate conclusion. But in this digression he considers it proper to introduce some inferential topics, unconnected with the cause and with the decision itself, which contain some praise of the speaker himself, or some vituperation of the adversary, or else may lead to some other topic from which he may derive some confirmation or reprehension, not by arguing, but by expanding the subject by some amplification or other. If any one thinks that this is a proper part of an oration, he may follow Hermagoras. For precepts for embellishing, and praising, and blaming, have partly been already given by us, and partly will be given hereafter in their proper place. But we do not think it right that this part should be classed among the regular divisions of a speech, because it appears improper that there should be digressions, except to some common topics, concerning which subject we must speak subsequently. But it does not seem desirable to handle praise and vituperation separately, but it seems better that they should be considered as forming part of the argumentation itself. At present we will treat of the conclusion of an oration.

LII. The conclusion is the end and terminating of the whole oration. It has three parts,—enumeration, indignation, and complaint. Enumeration is that by which matters which have been related in a scattered and diffuse manner are collected together, and, for the sake of recollecting them, are brought under our view. If this is always treated in the same manner, it will be completely evident to every one that it is being handled according to some artificial system; but if it be done in many various ways, the orator will be able to escape this suspicion, and will not cause such weariness. Wherefore it will be desirable to act in the way which most people adopt, on account of its easiness; that is, to touch on each topic separately, and in that manner briefly to run over all sorts of argumentation; and also (which is, however, more difficult) to recount what portions of the subject you previously mentioned in the arrangement of the subject, as those which you promised to explain; and also to bring to the recollection of your hearers the reasonings by which you established each separate point, and then to ask of those who are hearing you what it is which they ought to wish to be proved to them; in this way:—"We proved this; we made that plain;" and by this means the hearer will recover his recollection of it, and will think that there is nothing besides which he ought to require.

And in these kinds of conclusions, as has been said before, it will be serviceable both to run over the arguments which you yourself have employed separately, and also (which is a matter requiring still greater art) to unite the opposite arguments with your own; and to show how completely you have done away with the arguments which were brought against you. And so, by a brief comparison, the recollection of the hearer will be refreshed both as to the confirmation which you adduced, and as to the reprehension which you employed. And it will be useful to vary these proceedings by other methods of pleading also. But you may carry on the enumeration in your own person, so as to remind your hearers of what you said, and in what part of your speech you said each thing; and also you may bring on the stage some other character, or some different circumstance, and then make your whole enumeration with reference to that. If it is a person, in this way:—"For if the framer of the law were to appear, and were to inquire of you why you doubted, what could you say after this, and this, and this has been proved to you?" And in this case, as also in our own character, it will be in our power to run over all kinds of argumentation separately: and at one time to refer all separate genera to different classes of the division, and at another to ask of the hearer what he requires, and at another to adopt a similar course by a comparison of one's own arguments and those of the opposite party.

But a different class of circumstance will be introduced if an enumerative oration be connected with any subject of this sort,—law, place, city, or monument, in this manner.—"What if the laws themselves could speak? Would not they also address this complaint to you? What more do you require, O judges when this, and this, and this has been already made plain to you?" And in this kind of argument it is allowable to use all these same methods. But this is given as a common precept to guide one in framing an enumeration, that out of every part of the argument, since the whole cannot be repeated over again, that is to be selected which is of the greatest weight, and that each point is to be run over as briefly as possible, so that it shall appear to be only a refreshing of the recollection of the hearers, not a repetition of the speech.

LIII. Indignation is a kind of speech by which the effect produced is, that great hatred is excited against a man, or great dislike of some proceeding is originated. In an address of this kind we wish to have this understood first, that it is possible to give vent to indignation from all those topics which we have suggested in laying down precepts for the confirmation of a speech. For any amplifications whatever, and every sort of indignation may be expressed, derived from those circumstances which are attributed to persons and to things, but still we had better consider those precepts which can be laid down separately with respect to indignation.

The first topic is derived from authority, when we relate what a great subject of anxiety that affair has been to the immortal gods, or to those whose authority ought to carry the greatest weight with it. And that topic will be derived from prophecies, from oracles, from prophets, from tokens, from prodigies, from answers, and from other things like these. Also from our ancestors, from kings, from states, from nations from the wisest men, from the senate, the people, the framers of laws. The second topic is that by which it is shown with amplification, by means of indignation, whom that affair concerns,— whether it concerns all men or the greater part of men, (which is a most serious business,) or whether it concerns the higher classes, such as those men are on whose authority the indignation which we are professing is grounded, (which is most scandalous,) or whether it affects those men who are one's equals in courage, and fortune, and personal advantages, (which is most iniquitous,) or whether it affects our inferiors, (which is most arrogant).

The third topic is that which we employ when we are inquiring what is likely to happen, if every one else acts in the same manner. And at the same time we point out if this man is permitted to act thus, that there will be many imitators of the same audacity, and then from that we shall be able to point out how much evil will follow.

The fourth topic is one by the use of which we show that many men are eagerly looking out to see what is decided, in order that they may be able to see by the precedent of what is allowed to one, what will be allowed to themselves also in similar circumstances.

The fifth topic is one by the use of which we show that everything else which has been badly managed, as soon as the truth concerning them is ascertained, may be all set right, that this thing, however, is one which, if it be once decided wrongly, cannot be altered by any decision, nor set right by any power.

The sixth topic is one by which the action spoken of is proved to have been done designedly and on purpose, and then we add this argument, that pardon ought not to be granted to an intentional crime.

The seventh topic is one which we employ when we say that any deed is foul, and cruel, and nefarious, and tyrannical; that it has been effected by violence or by the influence of riches—a thing which is as remote as possible from the laws and from all ideas of equal justice.

LIV. An eighth topic is one of which we avail ourselves to demonstrate that the crime which is the present subject of discussion is not a common one,—not one such as is often perpetrated. And, that is foreign to the nature of even men in a savage state, of the most barbarous nations, or even of brute beasts. Actions of this nature are such as are wrought with cruelty towards one's parents, or wife, or husband, or children, or relations, or suppliants; next to them, if anything has been done with inhumanity towards a man's elders,—towards those connected with one by ties of hospitality,—towards one's neighbours or one's friends,—to those with whom one has been in the habit of passing one's life,—to those by whom one has been brought up,—to those by whom one has been taught,—to the dead,—to those who are miserable and deserving of pity,—to men who are illustrious, noble, and who have been invested with honours and offices,—to those who have neither had power to injure another nor to defend themselves, such as boys, old men, women: by all which circumstances indignation is violently excited, and will be able to awaken the greatest hatred against a man who has injured any of these persons.

The ninth topic is one by which the action which is the subject of the present discussion is compared with others which are admitted on all hands to be offences. And in that way it is shown by comparison how much more atrocious and scandalous is the action which is the present subject of discussion.

The tenth topic is one by which we collect all the circumstances which have taken place in the performance of this action, and which have followed since that action, with great indignation at and reproach of each separate item, and by our description we bring the case as far as possible before the eyes of the judge before whom we are speaking, so that that which is scandalous may appear quite as scandalous to him as if he himself had been present to see what was done.

The eleventh topic is one which we avail ourselves of when we are desirous to show that the action has been done by him whom of all men in the world it least became to do it, and by whom indeed it ought to have been prevented if any one else had endeavoured to do it.

The twelfth topic is one by means of which we express our indignation that we should be the first people to whom this has happened, and that it has never occurred in any other instance.

The thirteenth topic is when insult is shown to have been added to injury, and by this topic we awaken hatred against pride and arrogance.

The fourteenth topic is one which we avail ourselves of to entreat those who hear us to consider our injuries as if they affected themselves; if they concern our children, to think of their own, if our wives have been injured, to recollect their own wives, if it is our aged relations who have suffered, to remember their own fathers or ancestors.

The fifteenth topic is one by which we say that those things which have happened to us appear scandalous even to foes and enemies, and as a general rule, indignation is derived from one or other of these topics.

LV. But complaint will usually take its origin from things of this kind. Complaint is a speech seeking to move the pity of the hearers. In this it is necessary in the first place to render the disposition of the hearer gentle and merciful, in order that it may the more easily be influenced by pity. And it will be desirable to produce that effect by common topics, such as those by which the power of fortune over all men is shown, and the weakness of men too is displayed, and if such an argument is argued with dignity and with impressive language, then the minds of men are greatly softened, and prepared to feel pity, while they consider their own weakness in the contemplation of the misfortunes of another.

Then the first topic to raise pity is that by which we show how great the prosperity of our clients was, and how great their present misery is.

The second is one which is divided according to different periods, according to which it is shown in what miseries they have been, and still are, and are likely to be hereafter.

The third topic is that by which each separate inconvenience is deplored, as, for instance, in speaking of the death of a man's son, the delight which the father took in his childhood, his love for him, his hope of him, the comfort he derived from him, the pains he took in his bringing up, and all other instances of the same sort, may be mentioned so as to exaggerate the complaint.

The fourth topic is one in which all circumstances which are discreditable or low or mean are brought forward, all circumstances which are unworthy of a man's age, or both, or fortune, or former honours or services, all the disasters which they have suffered or are liable to suffer.

The fifth topic is that by using which all disadvantages we brought separately before the eyes of the hearer, so that he who hears of them may seem to see them, and by the very facts themselves, and not only by the description of them, may be moved to pity as if he had been actually present.

The sixth topic is one by which the person spoken of is shown to be miserable, when he had no reason to expect any such fate; and that when he was expecting something else, he not only failed to obtain it, but fell into the most terrible misfortunes.

The seventh is one by which we suppose the fact of a similar mischance befalling the men who are listening to us, and require of them when they behold us to call to mind their own children, or their parents, or some one for whom they are bound to entertain affections.

The eighth is one by which something is said to have been done which ought not to have been done; or not to have been done which ought to have been. In this manner:—"I was not present, I did not see him, I did not hear his last words, I did not receive his last breath. Moreover, he died amid his enemies, he lay shamefully unburied in an enemy's country, being torn to pieces by wild beasts, and was deprived in death of even that honour which is the due of all men."

The ninth is one by which our speech is made to refer to things which are void both of language and sense; as if you were to adapt your discourse to a horse, a house, or a garment; by which topics the minds of those who are hearing, and who have been attached to any one, are greatly moved.

The tenth is one by which want, or weakness, or the desolate condition of any one is pointed out.

The eleventh is one in which is contained a recommendation to bury one's children, or one's parents, or one's own body, or to do any other such thing.

The twelfth is one in which a separation is lamented when you are separated from any one with whom you have lived most pleasantly,—as from a parent, a son, a brother, an intimate friend.

The thirteenth is one used when we complain with great indignation that we are ill-treated by those by whom above all others we least ought to be so,—as by our relations, or by friends whom we have served, and whom we have expected to be assistants to us; or by whom it is a shameful thing to be ill-treated,—as by slaves, or freedmen, or clients, or suppliants.

The fourteenth is one which is taken as an entreaty, in which those who hear us are entreated, in a humble and suppliant oration, to have pity on us.

The fifteenth is one in which we show that we are complaining not only of our own fortunes, but of those who ought to be dear to us.

The sixteenth is one by using which we show that our hearts are full of pity for others; and yet give tokens at the same time that it will be a great and lofty mind, and one able to endure disaster if any such should befall us. For often virtue and splendour, in which there is naturally great influence and authority, have more effect in exciting pity than humility and entreaties. And when men's minds are moved it will not be right to dwell longer on complaints; for, as Apollonius the rhetorician said, "Nothing dries quicker than a tear."

But since we have already, as it seems, said enough of all the different parts of a speech, and since this volume has swelled to a great size, what follows next shall be stated in the second book.

* * * * *

THE SECOND BOOK OF THE RHETORIC,

OR OF THE

TREATISE ON RHETORICAL INVENTION, OF M. T. CICERO.

I. Some men of Crotona, when they were rich in all kinds of resources, and when they were considered among the most prosperous people in Italy, were desirous to enrich the temple of Juno, which they regarded with the most religious veneration, with splendid pictures. Therefore they hired Zeuxis of Heraclea at a vast price, who was at that time considered to be far superior to all other painters, and employed him in that business. He painted many other pictures, of which some portion, on account of the great respect in which the temple is held, has remained to within our recollection; and in order that one of his mute representations might contain the preeminent beauty of the female form, he said that he wished to paint a likeness of Helen. And the men of Crotona, who had frequently heard that he excelled all other men in painting women, were very glad to hear this; for they thought that if he took the greatest pains in that class of work in which he had the greatest skill, he would leave them a most noble work in that temple.

Nor were they deceived in that expectation: for Zeuxis immediately asked of them what beautiful virgins they had; and they immediately led him into the palaestra, and there showed him numbers of boys of the highest birth and of the greatest beauty. For indeed, there was a time when the people of Crotona were far superior to all other cities in the strength and beauty of their persons; and they brought home the most honourable victories from the gymnastic contests, with the greatest credit. While, therefore, he was admiring the figures of the boys and their personal perfection very greatly; "The sisters," say they, "of these boys are virgins in our city, so that how great their beauty is you may infer from these boys." "Give me, then," said he, "I beg you, the most beautiful of these virgins, while I paint the picture which I promised you, so that the reality may be transferred from the breathing model to the mute likeness." Then the citizens of Crotona, in accordance with a public vote, collected the virgins into one place, and gave the painter the opportunity of selecting whom he chose. But he selected five, whose names many poets have handed down to tradition, because they had been approved by the judgment of the man who was bound to have the most accurate judgment respecting beauty. For he did not think that he could find all the component parts of perfect beauty in one person, because nature has made nothing of any class absolutely perfect in every part. Therefore, as if nature would not have enough to give to everybody if it had given everything to one, it balances one advantage bestowed upon a person by another disadvantage.

II. But since the inclination has arisen in my mind to write a treatise on the art of speaking, we have not put forth any single model of which every portion was necessarily to be copied by us, of whatever sort they might be; but, having collected together all the writers on the subject into one place, we have selected what each appears to have recommended which may be most serviceable, and we have thus culled the flower from various geniuses. For of those who are worthy of fame or recollection, there is no one who appears either to have said nothing well, or everything admirably. So that it seemed folly either to forsake the sensible maxims brought forward by any one, merely because we are offended at some other blunder of his, or, on the other hand, to embrace his faults because we have been tempted by some sensible precept which he has also delivered.

But if in other pursuits also men would select all that was found most sensible from many sources, instead of devoting themselves to one fixed leader, they would err less on the side of arrogance; they would not persist so much in error, and they would make less enormous mistakes through ignorance. And if we had as deep an acquaintance with this art as he had with that of painting, perhaps this work of ours might appear as admirable in its kind as his picture did. For we have had an opportunity of selecting from a much more copious store of models than he had. He was able to make his selection from one city, and from that number of virgins only which existed at that time and place; but we have had opportunity of making our selection from all the men who have ever lived from the very first beginning of this science, being reduced to a system up to the present day, and taking whatever we thought worth while from all the stores which lay open before us.

And Aristotle, indeed, has collected together all the ancient writers on this art, from the first writer on the subject and inventor of it, Tisias, and has compiled with great perspicuity the precepts of each of them, mentioning them by name, after having sought them out with exceeding care; and he has disentangled them with great diligence and explained their difficulties; and he has so greatly excelled the original writers themselves in suavity and brevity of diction, that no one is acquainted with their precepts from their own writings, but all who wish to know what maxims they have laid down, come back to him as to a far more agreeable expounder of their meaning.

And he himself has set before us himself and those too who had lived before his time, in order that we might be acquainted with the method of others, and with his own. And those who have followed him, although they have expended a great deal of labour on the most profound and important portions of philosophy, as he himself also, whose example they were following, had done, have still left us many precepts on the subject of speaking. And other masters of this science have also come forward, taking their rise, as it were in other springs, who have also been of great assistance in eloquence, as far at least as artificial rules can do any good. For there lived at the same time as Aristotle, a great and illustrious rhetorician, named Isocrates, though we have not entirely discovered what his system was.

But we have found many lessons respecting their art from his pupils and from those who proceeded immediately afterwards from this school.

III. From these two different families, as it were, the one of which, while it was chiefly occupied with philosophy, still devoted some portion of its attention to the rhetorical science, and the other was wholly absorbed in the study and teaching of eloquence, but both kinds of study were united by their successors, who brought to the aid of their own pursuits those things which appeared to have been profitably said by either of them, and those and the others their predecessors are the men whom we and all our countrymen have proposed to ourselves as models, as far as we were able to make them so, and we have also contributed something from our own stores to the common stock.

But if the things which are set forth in these books deserved to be selected with such great eagerness and care as they were, then certainly, neither we ourselves nor others will repent of our industry. But if we appear either rashly to have passed over some doctrine of some one worth noticing, or to have adopted it without sufficient elegance, in that case when we are taught better by some one, we will easily and cheerfully change our opinion. For what is discreditable is, not the knowing little, but the persisting foolishly and long in what one does not understand, because the one thing is attributed to the common infirmity of man, but the other to the especial fault of the individual.

Wherefore we, without affirming anything positively, but making inquiry at the same time, will advance each position with some doubt, lest while we gain this trifling point of being supposed to have written this treatise with tolerable neatness, we should lose that which is of the greater importance, the credit, namely, of not adopting any idea rashly and arrogantly. But this we shall endeavour to gain both at present and during the whole course of our life with great care, as far as our abilities will enable us to do so. But at present, lest we should appear to be too prolix, we will speak of the other points which it seems desirable to insist on.

Therefore, while we were explaining the proper classification of this art, and its duties, and its object, and its subject matter, and its divisions, the first book contained an account of the different kinds of disputes, and inventions, and statements of cases, and decisions. After that, the parts of a speech were described, and all necessary precepts for all of them were laid down. So that we not only discussed other topics in that book with tolerable distinctness, we spoke at that same time in a more scattered manner of the topics of confirmation and reprehension; and at present we think it best to give certain topics for confirming and reprehending, suited to every class of causes. And because it has been explained with some diligence in the former book, in what manner argumentations ought to be handled, in this book it will be sufficient to set forth the arguments which have been discovered for each kind of subject simply, and without any embellishment, so that, in this book, the arguments themselves may be found, and in the former, the proper method of polishing them. So that the reader must refer the precepts which are now laid down, to the topics of confirmation and reprehension.

IV. Every discussion, whether demonstrative, or deliberative, or judicial, must be conversant with some kind or other of statement of the case which has been explained in the former book; sometimes with one, sometimes with several. And though this is the case, still as some things can be laid down in a general way respecting everything, there are also other rules and different methods separately laid down for each particular kind of discussion. For praise, or blame, or the statement of an opinion, or accusation, or denial, ought all to effect different ends. In judicial investigations the object of inquiry is, what is just, in demonstrative discussion the question is what is honourable, in deliberations, in our opinion, what we inquire is, what is honourable and at the same time expedient. For the other writers on this subject have thought it right to limit the consideration of expediency to speeches directed to persuasion or dissuasion.

Those kinds of discussions then whose objects and results are different, cannot be governed by the same precepts. Not that we are saying now that the same statement of the case is not admissible in all of them, but some kinds of speech arise from the object and kind of the discussion, if it refers to the demonstration of some kind of life, or to the delivery of some opinion. Wherefore now, in explaining controversies, we shall have to deal with causes and precepts of a judicial kind, from which many precepts also which concern similar disputes will be transferred to other kinds of causes without much difficulty. But hereafter we will speak separately of each kind.

At present we will begin with the conjectural statement of a case of which this example may be sufficient to be given—A man overtook another on his journey as he was going on some commercial expedition, and carrying a sum of money with him, he, as men often do entered into conversation with him on the way, the result of which was, that they both proceeded together with some degree of friendship, so that when they had arrived at the same inn, they proposed to sup together and to sleep in the same apartment. Having supped, they retired to rest in the same place. But when the innkeeper (for that is what is said to have been discovered since, after the man had been detected in another crime) had taken notice of one of them, that is to say, of him who had the money, he came by night, after he had ascertained that they were both sound asleep, as men usually are when tired, and took from its sheath the sword of the one who had not the money, and which sword he had lying by his side and slew the other man with it and took away his money, and replaced the bloody sword in the sheath, and returned himself to his bed.

But the man with whose sword the murder had been committed, rose long before dawn and called over and over again on his companion; he thought that he did not answer because he was overcome with sleep; and so he took his sword and the rest of the things which he had with him, and departed on his journey alone. The innkeeper not long afterwards raised an outcry that the man was murdered, and in company with some of his lodgers pursued the man who had gone away. They arrest him on his journey, draw his sword out of its sheath, and find it bloody, the man is brought back to the city by them, and put on his trial. On this comes the allegation of the crime, "You murdered him," and the denial, "I did not murder him," and from this is collected the statement of the case. The question in the conjectural examination is the same as that submitted to the judges, "Did he murder him, or not?"

V. Now we will set forth the topics one portion of which applies to all conjectural discussion. But it will be desirable to take notice of this in the exposition of these topics and of all the others, and to observe that they do not all apply to every discussion. For as every man's name is made up of some letters, and not of every letter, so it is not every store of arguments which applies to every argumentation, but some portion which is necessary applies to each. All conjecture, then, must be derived either from the cause of an action, or from the person, or from the case itself.

The cause of an action is divided into impulsion and ratiocination. Impulsion is that which without thought encourages a man to act in such and such a manner, by means of producing some affection of the mind, as love, anger, melancholy, fondness for wine, or indeed anything by which the mind appears to be so affected as to be unable to examine anything with deliberation and care, and to do what it does owing to some impulse of the mind, rather than in consequence of any deliberate purpose.

But ratiocination is a diligent and careful consideration of whether we shall do anything or not do it. And it is said to have been in operation, when the mind appears for some particular definite reason to have avoided something which ought not to have been done, or to have adopted something which ought to have been done, so that if anything is said to have been done for the sake of friendship, or of chastising an enemy, or under the influence of fear, or of a desire for glory or for money, or in short, to comprise everything under one brief general head, for the sake of retaining, or increasing, or obtaining any advantage; or, on the other hand, for the purpose of repelling, or diminishing, or avoiding any disadvantage;—for those former things must fall under one or other of those heads, if either any inconvenience is submitted to for the purpose of avoiding any greater inconvenience, or of obtaining any more important advantage; or if any advantage is passed by for the sake of obtaining some other still greater advantage, or of avoiding some more important disadvantage.

This topic is as it were a sort of foundation of this statement of the case; for nothing that is done is approved of by any one unless some reason be shown why it has been done. Therefore the accuser, when he says that anything has been done in compliance with some impulse, ought to exaggerate that impulse, and any other agitation or affection of the mind, with all the power of language and variety of sentiments of which he is master, and to show how great the power of love is, how great the agitation of mind which arises from anger, or from any one of those causes which he says was that which impelled any one to do anything. And here we must take care, by an enumeration of examples of men who have done anything under the influence of similar impulse, and by a collation of similar cases, and by an explanation of the way in which the mind itself is affected, to hinder its appearing marvellous if the mind of a man has been instigated by such influence to some pernicious or criminal action.

VI. But when the orator says that any one has done such and such an action, not through impulse, but in consequence of deliberate reasoning, he will then point out what advantage he has aimed at, or what inconvenience he has avoided, and he will exaggerate the influence of those motives as much as he can, so that as far as possible the cause which led the person spoken of to do wrong, may appear to have been an adequate one. If it was for the sake of glory that he did so and so, then he will point out what glory he thought would result from it; again, if he was influenced by desire of power, or riches, or by friendship, or by enmity; and altogether whatever the motive was, which he says was his inducement to the action, he will exaggerate as much as possible.

And he is bound to give great attention to this point, not only what the effect would have been in reality, but still more what it would have been in the opinion of the man whom he is accusing. For it makes no difference that there really was or was not any advantage or disadvantage, if the man who is accused believed that there would or would not be such. For opinion deceives men in two ways, when either the matter itself is of a different kind from that which it is believed to be, or when the result is not such as they thought it would be. The matter itself is of a different sort when they think that which is good bad, or, on the other hand, when they think that good which is bad. Or when they think that good or bad which is neither good nor bad, or when they think that which is good or bad neither bad nor good.

Now that this is understood, if any one denies that there is any money more precious or sweeter to a man than his brother's or his friend's life, or even than his own duty, the accuser is not to deny that; for then the blame and the chief part of the hatred will be transferred to him who denies that which is said so truly and so piously. But what he ought to say is, that the man did not think so; and that assertion must be derived from those topics which relate to the person, concerning whom we must speak hereafter.

VII. But the result deceives a person, when a thing has a different result from that which the persons who are accused are said to have thought it would have. As when a man is said to have slain a different person from him whom he intended to slay, either because he was deceived by the likeness or by some suspicion, or by some false indication; or that he slew a man who had not left him his heir in his will, because he believed that he had left him his heir. For it is not right to judge of a man's belief by the result, but rather to consider with what expectation, and intention, and hope he proceeded to such a crime; and to recollect that the matter of real importance is to consider with what intention a man does a thing, and not what the consequence of his action turns out to be.

And in this topic this will be the great point for the accuser, if he is able to show that no one else had any reason for doing so at all. And the thing next in importance will be to show that no one else had such great or sufficient reason for doing so. But if others appear also to have had a motive for doing so, then we must show that they had either no power, or no opportunity, or no inclination to do it. They had no power if it can be said that they did not know it, or were not in the place, or were unable to have accomplished it; they had no opportunity, if it can be proved that any plan, any assistants, any instruments, and all other things which relate to such an action, were wanting to them. They had no inclination, if their disposition can be said to be entirely alien to such conduct, and unimpeachable. Lastly, whatever arguments we allow a man on his trial to use in his defence, the very same the prosecutor will employ in delivering others from blame. But that must be done with brevity, and many arguments must be compressed into one, in order that he may not appear to be accusing the man on his trial for the sake of defending some one else, but to be defending some one else with a view to strengthen his accusation against him.

VIII. And these are for the most part the things which must be done and considered by an accuser. But the advocate for the defence will say, on the other hand, either that there was no motive at all, or, if he admits that there was, he will make light of it, and show that it was a very slight one, or that such conduct does not often proceed from such a motive. And with reference to this topic it will be necessary to point out what is the power and character of that motive, by which the person on his trial is said to have been induced to commit any action; and in doing this it is requisite to adduce instances and examples of similar cases, and the actual nature of such a motive is to be explained as gently as possible, so that the circumstance which is the subject of the discussion may be explained away, and instead of being considered as a cruel and disorderly act, may be represented as something more mild and considerate, and still the speech itself may be adapted to the mind of the hearer, and to a sort of inner feeling, as it were, in his mind.

But the orator will weaken the suspicions arising from the ratiocination, if he shall say either that the advantage intimated had no existence, or a very slight one, or that it was a greater one to others, or that it was no greater advantage to himself than to others, or that it was a greater disadvantage than advantage to himself. So that the magnitude of the advantage which is said to have been desired, was not to be compared with the disadvantage which was really sustained, or with the danger which was incurred. And all those topics will be handled in the same manner in speaking of the avoiding of disadvantage.

But if the prosecutor has said that the man on his trial was pursuing what appeared to him to be an advantage, or was avoiding that which appeared to him to be a disadvantage, even though he was mistaken in that opinion, then the advocate for the defence must show that no one can be so foolish as to be ignorant of the truth in such an affair. And if that be granted, then the other position cannot be granted, that the man ever doubted at all what the case was, but that he, without the least hesitation, considered what was false as false, and what was true as true. But if he doubted, then it was a proof of absolute insanity for a man under the influence of a doubtful hope to incur a certain danger.

But as the accuser when he is seeking to remove the guilt from others must use the topics proper to an advocate for the defence; so the man on his trial must use those topics which have been allotted to an accuser, when he wishes to transfer an accusation from his own shoulders to those of others.

IX. But conjectures will be derived from the person, if those things which have been attributed to persons are diligently considered, all of which we have mentioned in the first book; for sometimes some suspicion arises from the name. But when we say the name, we mean also the surname. For the question is about the particular and peculiar name of a man, as if we were to say that a man is called Caldus because he is a man of a hasty and sudden disposition; or that ignorant Greeks have been deceived by men being called Clodius, or Caecilius, or Marcus.

And we may also derive some suspicious circumstances from nature; for all these questions, whether it is a man or a woman, whether he is of this state or that one, of what ancestors a man is descended, who are his relations, what is his age, what is his disposition, what bodily strength, or figure, or constitution he has, which are all portions of a man's nature, have much influence in leading men to form conjectures.

Many suspicions also are engendered by men's way of life, when the inquiry is how, and by whom, and among whom a man was brought up and educated, and with whom he associates, and what system and habits of domestic life he is devoted to.

Moreover, argumentation often arises from fortune; when we consider whether a man is a slave or a free man, rich or poor, noble or ignoble, prosperous or unfortunate; whether he now is, or has been, or is likely to be a private individual or a magistrate; or, in fact, when any one of those circumstances is sought to be ascertained which are attributable to fortune. But as habit consists in some perfect and consistent formation of mind or body, of which kind are virtue, knowledge, and their contraries; the fact itself, when the whole circumstances are stated, will show whether this topic affords any ground for suspicion. For the consideration of the state of a man's mind is apt to give good grounds for conjecture, as of his affectionate or passionate disposition, or of any annoyance to which he has been exposed; because the power of all such feelings and circumstances is well understood, and what results ensue after any one of them is very easy to be known.

But since study is an assiduous and earnest application of the mind to any particular object with intense desire, that argument which the case itself requires will easily be deduced from it. And again, some suspicion will be able to be inferred from the intention; for intention is a deliberate determination of doing or not doing something. And after this it will be easy to see with respect to facts, and events, and speeches, which are divided into three separate times, whether they contribute anything to confirming the conjectures already formed in the way of suspicion.

X. And those things indeed are attributed to persons, which when they are all collected together in one place, it will be the business of the accuser to use them as inducing a disapprobation of the person; for the fact itself has but little force unless the disposition of the man who is accused can be brought under such suspicion as to appear not to be inconsistent with such a fault. For although there is no great advantage in expressing disapprobation of any one's disposition, when there is no cause why he should have done wrong, still it is but a trifling thing that there should be a motive for an offence, if the man's disposition is proved to be inclined to no line of conduct which is at all discreditable. Therefore the accuser ought to bring into discredit the life of the man whom he is accusing, by reference to his previous actions, and to show whether he has ever been previously convicted of a similar offence. And if he cannot show that, he must show whether he has ever incurred the suspicion of any similar guilt; and especially, if possible, that he has committed some offence or other of some kind under the influence of some similar motive to this which is in existence here, in some similar case, or in an equally important case, or in one more important, or in one less important. As, if with respect to a man who he says has been induced by money to act in such and such a manner, he were able to show that any other action of his in any case had been prompted by avarice.

And again it will be desirable in every cause to mention the nature, or the manner of life, or the pursuits, or the fortune, or some one of those circumstances which are attributed to persons, in connexion with that cause which the speaker says was the motive which induced the man on his trial to do wrong; and also, if one cannot impute anything to him in respect of an exactly corresponding class of faults, to bring the disposition of one's adversary into discredit by reference to some very dissimilar class. As, if you were to accuse him of having done so and so, because he was instigated by avarice; and yet, if you are unable to show that the man whom you accuse is avaricious, you must show that other vices are not wholly foreign to his nature, and that on that account it is no great wonder if a man who in any affair has behaved basely, or covetously, or petulantly, should have erred in this business also. For in proportion as you can detract from the honesty and authority of the man who is accused, in the same proportion has the force of the whole defence been weakened.

If it cannot be shown that the person on his trial has been ever before implicated in any previous guilt, then that topic will come into play which we are to use for the purpose of encouraging the judges to think that the former character of the man has no bearing on the present question; for that he has formerly concealed his wickedness, but that he is now manifestly convicted; so that it is not proper that this case should be looked at with reference to his former life, but that his former life should now be reproved by this conduct of his, and that formerly he had either no opportunity of doing wrong, or no motive to do so. Or if this cannot be said, then we must have recourse to this last assertion,—that it is no wonder if he now does wrong for the first time, for that it is necessary that a man who wishes to commit sin, must some time or other commit it for the first time. If nothing whatever is known of his previous life, then it is best to pass over this topic, and to state the reason why it is passed over, and then to proceed at once to corroborate the accusation by arguments.

XI. But the advocate for the defence ought in the first place to show, if he can, that the life of the person who is accused has always been as honourable as possible. And he will do this best by recounting any well known services which he has rendered to the state in general, or any that he has done to his parents, or relations, or friends, or kinsmen, or associates, or even any which are more remarkable or more unusual, especially if they have been done with any extraordinary labour, or danger, or both, or when there was no absolute necessity, purely because it was his duty, or if he has done any great benefit to the republic, or to his parents, or to any other of the people whom I have just mentioned, and if, too, he can show that he has never been so influenced by any covetousness as to abandon his duty, or to commit any error of any description. And this statement will be the more confirmed, if when it is said that he had an opportunity of doing something which was not quite creditable with impunity, it can be shown at the same time that he had no inclination to do it.

But this very kind of argument will be all the stronger if the person on his trial can be shown to have been unimpeachable previously in that particular sort of conduct of which he is now accused, as, for instance, if he be accused of having done so and so for the sake of avarice, and can be proved to have been all his life utterly indifferent to the acquisition of money. On this indignation may be expressed with great weight, united with a complaint that it is a most miserable thing, and it may be argued that it is a most scandalous thing, to think that that was the man's motive, when his disposition during the whole of his life has been as unlike it as possible. Such a motive often harries audacious men into guilt, but it has no power to impel an upright man to sin. It is unjust, moreover, and injurious to every virtuous man, that a previously well-spent life should not be of the greatest possible advantage to a man at such a time, but that a decision should be come to with reference only to a sudden accusation which can be got up in a hurry, and with no reference to a man's previous course of life, which cannot be extemporised to suit an occasion, and which cannot be altered by any means.

But if there have been any acts of baseness in his previous life, or if they be said to have undeservedly acquired such a reputation, or if his actions are to be attributed by the envy, or love of detraction, or mistaken opinion of some people, either to ignorance, or necessity, or to the persuasion of young men, or to any other affection of mind in which there is no vice, or if he has been tainted with errors of a different kind, so that his disposition appears not entirely faultless, but still far remote from such a fault, and if his disgraceful or infamous course of life cannot possibly be mitigated by any speech,—then it will be proper to say that the inquiry does not concern his life and habits, but is about that crime for which he is now prosecuted, so that, omitting all former actions, it is proper that the matter which is in hand should be attended to.

XII. But suspicions may be derived from the fact itself, if the administration of the whole matter is examined into in all its parts; and these suspicions will arise partly from the affair itself when viewed separately, and partly from the persons and the affairs taken together. They will be able to be derived from the affair, if we diligently consider those circumstances which have been attributed to such affairs. And from them all the different genera, and most subordinate species, will appear to be collected together in this statement of the case.

It will therefore be desirable to consider in the first place what circumstances there are which are united to the affair itself,—that is to say, which cannot be separated from it, and with reference to this topic it will be sufficient to consider what was done before the affair in question took place from which a hope arose of accomplishing it, and an opportunity was sought of doing it, what happened with respect to the affair itself, and what ensued afterwards. In the next place, the execution of the whole affair must be dealt with for this class of circumstances which have been attributed to the affair has been discussed in the second topic.

So with reference to this class of circumstances we must have a regard to time, place, occasion, and opportunity, the force of each particular of which has been already carefully explained when we were laying down precepts for the confirmation of an argument. Wherefore, that we may not appear to have given no rules respecting these things, and that we may not, on the other hand, appear to have repeated the same things twice over, we will briefly point out what it is proper should be considered in each part. In reference to place, then, opportunity is to be considered; and in reference to time, remoteness; and in reference to occasion, the convenience suitable for doing anything; and with reference to facility, the store and abundance of those things by means of which anything is done more easily, or without which it cannot be done at all.

In the next place we must consider what is added to the affair, that is to say, what is greater, what is less, what is equally great, what is similar. And from these topics some conjecture is derived, if proper consideration is given to the question how affairs of greater importance, or of less, or of equal magnitude, or of similar character, are usually transacted. And in this class of subjects the result also ought to be examined into; that is to say, what usually ensues as the consequence of every action must be carefully considered; as, for instance, fear, joy, trepidation.

But the fourth part was a necessary consequence from those circumstances which we said were attendant on affairs. In it those things are examined which follow the accomplishment of an affair, either immediately or after an interval. And in this examination we shall see whether there is any custom, any action, any system, or practice, or habit, any general approval or disapproval on the part of mankind in general, from which circumstance some suspicion at times arises.

XIII. But there are some suspicions which are derived from the circumstances which are attributed to persons and things taken together. For many circumstances arising from fortune, and from nature, and from the way of a man's life, and from his pursuits and actions, and from chance, or from speeches, or from a person's designs, or from his usual habit of mind or body, have reference to the same things which render a statement credible or incredible, and which are combined with a suspicion of the fact.

For it is above all things desirable that inquiry should be made in this way, of stating the case first of all, whether anything could be done; in the next place, whether it could have been done by any one else; then we consider the opportunity, on which we have spoken before; then whether what has been done is a crime which one is bound to repent of; we must inquire too whether he had any hope of concealing it; then whether there was any necessity for his doing so; and as to this we must inquire both whether it was necessary that the thing should be done at all, or that it should be done in that manner. And some portion of these considerations refer to the design, which has been already spoken of as what is attributed to persons; as in the instance of that cause which we have mentioned. These circumstances will be spoken of as before the affair,—the facts, I mean, of his having joined himself to him so intimately on the march, of his having sought occasion to speak with him, of his having lodged with him, and supped with him. These circumstances were a part of the affair,—night, and sleep. These came after the affair,—the fact of his having departed by himself; of his having left his intimate companion with such indifference; of his having a bloody sword.

Part of these things refer to the design. For the question is asked, whether the plan of executing this deed appears to have been one carefully devised and considered, or whether it was adopted so hastily that it is not likely that any one should have gone on to crime so rashly. And in this inquiry we ask also whether the deed could have been done with equal ease in any other manner; or whether it could have happened by chance. For very often if there has been a want of money, or means, or assistants, there would not appear to have been any opportunity of doing such a deed. If we take careful notice in this way, we shall see that all these circumstances which are attributed to things, and those too which are attributed to persons, fit one another. In this case it is neither easy nor necessary, as it is in the former divisions, to draw distinctions as to how the accuser and how the advocate for the defence ought to handle each topic. It is not necessary, because, when the case is once stated, the circumstances themselves will teach those men, who do not expect to find everything imaginable in this treatise, what is suitable for each case; and they will apply a reasonable degree of understanding to the rules which are here laid down, in the way of comparing them with the systems of others. And it is not easy, because it would be an endless business to enter into a separate explanation with respect to every portion of every case; and besides, these circumstances are adapted to each part of the case in different manners on different occasions.

XIV. Wherefore it will be desirable to consider what we have now set forth. And our mind will approach invention with more ease, if it often and carefully goes over both its own relation and that of the opposite party, of what has been done; and if, eliciting what suspicions each part gives rise to, it considers why, and with what intention, and with what hopes and plans, each thing was done. Why it was done in this manner rather than in that; why by this man rather than by that; why it was done without any assistant, or why with this one; why no one was privy to it, or why somebody was, or why this particular person was; why this was done before; why this was not done before; why it was done in this particular instance; why it was done afterwards; what was done designedly, or what came as a consequence of the original action; whether the speech is consistent with the facts or with itself; whether this is a token of this thing, or of that thing, or of both this and that, and which it is a token of most; what has been done which ought not to have been done, or what has not been done which ought to have been done.

When the mind considers every portion of the whole business with this intention, then the topics which have been reserved, will come into use, which we have already spoken of; and certain arguments will be derived from them both separately and unitedly. Part of which arguments will depend on what is probable, part on what is necessary; there will be added also to conjecture questions, testimony, reports. All of which things each party ought to endeavour by a similar use of these rules to turn to the advantage of his own cause. For it will be desirable to suggest suspicions from questions, from evidence, and from some report or other, in the same manner as they have been derived from the cause, or the person, or the action.

Wherefore those men appear to us to be mistaken who think that this kind of suspicion does not need any regular system, and so do those who think that it is better to give rules in a different manner about the whole method of conjectural argument. For all conjecture must be derived from the same topics; for both the cause of every rumour and the truth of it will be found to arise from the things attributed to him who in his inquiry has made any particular statement, and to him who has done so in his evidence. But in every cause a part of the arguments is joined to that cause alone which is expressed, and it is derived from it in such a manner that it cannot be very conveniently transferred from it to all other causes of the same kind; but part of it is more rambling, and adapted either to all causes of the same kind, or at all events to most of them.

XV. These arguments then which can be transferred to many causes, we call common topics. For a common topic either contains some amplification of a well understood thing,—as if any one were desirous to show that a man who has murdered his father is worthy of the very extremity of punishment; and this topic is not to be used except when the cause has been proved and is being summed up;—or of a doubtful matter which has some probable arguments which can be produced on the other side of the question also; as a man may say that it is right to put confidence in suspicions, and, on the contrary, that it is not right to put confidence in suspicions. And a portion of the common topics is employed in indignation or in complaint, concerning which we have spoken already. A part is used in urging any probable reason on either side.

But an oration is chiefly distinguished and made plain by a sparing introduction of common topics, and by giving the hearers actual information by some topics, and by confirming previously used arguments in the same way. For it is allowable to say something common when any topic peculiar to the cause is introduced with care; and when the mind of the hearer is refreshed so as to be inclined to attend to what follows, or is reawakened by everything which has been already said. For all the embellishments of elocution, in which there is a great deal both of sweetness and gravity, and all things, too, which have any dignity in the invention of words or sentences, are bestowed upon common topics.

Wherefore there are not as many common topics for orators as there are for lawyers. For they cannot be handled with elegance and weight, as their nature requires, except by those who have acquired a great flow of words and ideas by constant practice. And this is enough for us to say in a general way concerning the entire class of common topics.

XVI. Now we will proceed to explain what common topics are usually available in a conjectural statement of a case. As for instance—that it is proper to place confidence in suspicions, or that it is not proper, that it is proper to believe witnesses, or that it is not proper, that it is proper to believe examinations, or that it is not proper, that it is proper to pay attention to the previous course of a man's life, or that it is not proper, that it is quite natural that a man who has done so and so should have committed this crime also, or that it is not natural, that it is especially necessary to consider the motive, or that it is not necessary. And all these common topics, and any others which arise out of any argument peculiar to the cause in hand, may be turned either way.

But there is one certain topic for an accuser by which he exaggerates the atrocity of an action, and there is another by which he says that it is not necessary to pity the miserable. That, too, is a topic for an advocate for the defence by which the false accusations of the accusers are shown up with indignation, and that by which pity is endeavoured to be excited by complaints. These and all other common topics are derived from the same rules from which the other systems of arguments proceed, but those are handled in a more delicate, and acute, and subtle manner, and these with more gravity, and more embellishment, and with carefully selected words and ideas. For in them the object is, that that which is stated may appear to be true. In these, although it is desirable to preserve the appearance of truth, still the main object is to give importance to the statement. Now let us pass on to another statement of the case.

XVII. When there is a dispute as to the name of a thing because the meaning of a name is to be defined by words, it is called a definitive statement. By way of giving an example of this, the following case may be adduced. Caius Flaminius, who as consul met with great disasters in the second Punic war, when he was tribune of the people, proposed, in a very seditious manner, an agrarian law to the people, against the consent of the senate, and altogether against the will of all the nobles. While he was holding an assembly of the people, his own father dragged him from the temple. He is impeached of treason. The charge is—"You attacked the majesty of the people in dragging down a tribune of the people from the temple." The denial is—"I did not attack the majesty of the people." The question is—"Whether he attacked the majesty of the people or not?" The argument is—"I only used the power which I legitimately had over my own son." The denial of this argument is—"But a man who, by the power belonging to him as a father, that is to say, as a private individual, attacks the power of a tribune of the people, that is to say, the power of the people itself, attacks the majesty of the people." The question for the judges is—"Whether a man attacks the majesty of the people who uses his power as a father in opposition to the power of a tribune?" And all the arguments must be brought to bear on this question.

And, that no one may suppose by any chance that we are not aware that some other statement of the case may perhaps be applicable to this cause, we are taking that portion only for which we are going to give rules. But when all parts have been explained in this book, any one, if he will only attend diligently, will see every sort of statement in every sort of cause, and all their parts, and all the discussions which are incidental to them. For we shall mention them all.

The first topic then for an accuser is a short and plain definition, and one in accordance with the general opinion of men, of that name, the meaning of which is the subject of inquiry. In this manner—"To attack the majesty of the people is to detract from the dignity, or the rank, or the power of the people, or of those men to whom the people has given power." This definition being thus briefly set forth in words, must be confirmed by many assertions and reasons and must be shown to be such as you have described it. Afterwards it will be desirable to add to the definition which you have given, the action of the man who is accused, and to add it too with reference to the character which you have proved it to have. Take for instance—"to attack the majesty of the people." You must show that the adversary does attack the majesty of the people, and you must confirm this whole topic by a common topic, by which the atrocity or indignity of the fact, and the whole guilt of it, and also our indignation at it, may be increased.

After that it will be desirable to invalidate the definition of the adversaries, but that will be invalidated if it be proved to be false. This proof must be deduced from the belief of men concerning it, when we consider in what manner and under what circumstances men are accustomed to use that expression in their ordinary writing or talking. It will also be invalidated if the proof of that description be shown to be discreditable or useless, and if it be shown what disadvantages will ensue if that position be once admitted. And it will be derived from the divisions of honour and usefulness, concerning which we will give rules when we lay down a system of deliberations. And if we compare the definition given by our adversaries with our own definition, and prove our own to be true, and honourable, and useful, and theirs to be entirely different. But we shall seek out things like them in an affair of either greater, or less, or equal importance, from which our description will be proved.

XVIII Now, if there be more matters to be defined,—as for instance, if we inquire whether he is a thief or a sacrilegious person who has stolen sacred vessels from a private house,—we shall have to employ many definitions, and then the whole cause will have to be dealt with on a similar principle. But it is a common topic to dwell on the wickedness of that man who endeavours to wrest to his own purposes not only the effect of things, but also the meaning of words, in order both to do as he pleases, and to call what he does by whatever name he likes.

Then the first topic to be used by an advocate for the defence, is also a brief and plain definition of a name, adopted in accordance with the opinion of men. In this way— To diminish the majesty of the people is to usurp some of the public powers when you are not invested with any office. And then the confirmation of this definition is derived from similar instances and similar principles. Afterwards comes the separation of one's own action from that definition. Then comes the common topic by which the expediency or honesty of the action is increased.

Then comes the reprehension of the definition of the opposite party, which is also derived from all the same topics as those which we have prescribed to the accuser. And afterwards other arguments will be adduced besides the common topic. But that will be a common topic for the advocate of the defence to use, by which he will express indignation that the accuser not only alters facts in order to bring him into danger, but that he attempts also to alter words. For those common topics which are assumed either for the purpose of demonstrating the falsehood of the accusations of the prosecutor, or for exciting pity, or for expressing indignation at an action, or for the purpose of deterring people from showing pity, are derived from the magnitude of the danger, not from the nature of the cause. Wherefore they are incidental not to every cause, but to every description of cause. We have made mention of them in speaking of the conjectural statement of a case, but we shall use induction when the cause requires.

XIX But when the pleading appears to require some translation, or to need any alteration, either because he is not pleading who ought to do so, or he is not pleading with the man he ought, or before the men whom he ought to have for hearers, or in accordance with the proper law, or under liability to the proper punishment, or in reference to the proper accusation, or at the proper time, it is then called a transferable statement of the case. We should require many examples of this if we were to inquire into every sort of translation, but because the principle on which the rules proceed is similar, we have no need of a superfluity of instances. And in our usual practice it happens from many causes that such translations occur but seldom. For many actions are prevented by the exceptions allowed by the praetors, and we have the civil law established in such a way that that man is sure to lose his cause who does not conduct it as he ought. So that those actions greatly depend on the state of the law. For there the exceptions are demanded, and an opportunity is allowed of conducting the cause in some manner, and every formula of private actions is arranged. But in actual trials they occur less frequently, and yet, if they ever do occur at all, they are such that by themselves they have less strength, but they are confirmed by the assumption of some other statement in addition to them. As in a certain trial which took place "When a certain person had been prosecuted for poisoning, and, because he was also accused of parricide, the trial was ordered to proceed out of its regular order, when in the accusation some charges were corroborated by witnesses and arguments, but the parricide was barely mentioned, it was proper for the advocate for the defence to dwell much and long on this circumstance, as, nothing whatever was proved respecting the death of the accused person's parent, and therefore that it was a scandalous thing to inflict that punishment on him which is inflicted on parricides, but that that must inevitably be the case if he were convicted, since that it is added as one of the counts of the indictment, and since it is on that account that the trial has been ordered to be taken out of its regular order. Therefore if it is not right that that punishment should be inflicted on the criminal, it is also not right that he should be convicted, since that punishment must inevitably follow a conviction." Here the advocate for the defence, by bringing the commutation of the punishment into his speech, according to the transferable class of topics, will invalidate the whole accusation. But he will also confirm the alteration by a conjectural statement of the case when employed in defending his client on the other charges.

XX But we may give an example of translation in a cause, in this way—When certain armed men had come for the purpose of committing violence, and armed men were also prepared on the other side, and when one of the armed men with his sword cut off the hand of a certain Roman knight who resisted his violence, the man whose hand had been cut off brings an action for the injury. The man against whom the action is brought pleads a demurrer before the praetor, without there being any prejudice to a man on trial for his life. The man who brings the action demands a trial on the simple fact, the man against whom the action is brought says that a demurrer ought to be added. The question is—"Shall the demurrer be allowed or not?" The reason is—"No, for it is not desirable in an action for damages that there should be any prejudged decision of a crime, such as is the subject of inquiry when assassins are on their trial." The arguments intended to invalidate this reason are—"The injuries are such that it is a shame that a decision should not be come to as early as possible." The thing to be decided is—"Whether the atrocity of the injuries is a sufficient reason why, while that point is before the tribunal, a previous decision should be given concerning some greater crime, concerning which a tribunal is prepared." And this is the example. But in every cause the question ought to be put to both parties, by whom, and by whose agency, and how, and when it is desirable that the action should be brought, or the decision given; or what ought to be decided concerning that matter.

That ought to be assumed from the divisions of the law, concerning which we must speak hereafter; and we then ought to argue as to what is usually done in similar cases, and to consider whether, in this instance, out of wickedness, one course is really adopted and another pretended; or whether the tribunal has been appointed and the action allowed to proceed through folly or necessity, because it could not be done in any other manner, or owing to an opportunity which offered for acting in such a manner; or whether it has been done rightly without any interruption of any sort. But it is a common topic to urge against the man who seeks to avail himself of a demurrer to an action, that he is fleeing from a decision and from punishment, because he has no confidence in the justice of his cause. And that, owing to the demurrer, everything will be in confusion, if matters are not conducted and brought into court as they ought to be; that is to say, if it is either pleaded against a man it ought not, or with an improper penalty, or with an improper charge, or at an improper time; and this principle applies to any confusion of every sort of tribunal. Those three statements of cases then, which are not susceptible of any decisions, must be treated in this manner. At present let us consider the question and its divisions on general principles.

XXI. When the fact and the name of the action in question is agreed upon, and when there is no dispute as to the character of the action to be commenced; then the effect, and the nature, and the character of the business is inquired into. We have already said, that there appear to be two divisions of this; one which relates to facts and one which relates to law. It is like this: "A certain person made a minor his heir, but the minor died before he had come into the property which was under the care of guardians. A dispute has arisen concerning the inheritance which came to the minor, between those who are the reversionary heirs of the father of the minor,—the possession belongs to the reversionary heirs." The first statement is that of the next of kin—"That money, concerning which he, whose next of kin we are, said nothing in his will, belongs to us." The reply is—"No, it belongs to us who are the reversionary heirs according to the will of his father." The thing to be inquired into is—To whom does it rightfully belong? The argument is—"For the father made a will for himself and for his son as long as the latter was a minor, wherefore it is quite clear that the things which belonged to the son are now ours, according to the will of the father." The argument to upset this is—"Aye, the father made his own will, and appointed you as reversionary heir, not to his son, but himself. Wherefore, nothing except what belonged to him himself can be yours by his will." The point to be determined is, whether any one can make a will to affect the property of his son who is a minor, or, whether the reversionary heirs of the father of the family himself, are not the heirs of his son also as long as he is a minor. And it is not foreign to the subject, (in order that I may not, on the one hand, omit to mention it, or, on the other, keep continually repeating it,) to mention a thing here which has a bearing on many questions. There are causes which have many reasons, though the grounds of the cause are simple, and that is the case when what has been done, or what is being defended, may appear right or natural on many different accounts, as in this very cause. For this further reason may be suggested by the heirs—"For there cannot be more heirs than one of one property, for causes quite dissimilar, nor has it ever happened, that one man was heir by will, and another by law, of the same property." This, again, is what will be replied, in order to invalidate this—"It is not one property only; because one part of it was the adventitious property of the minor, whose heir no one had been appointed by will at that time, in the case of anything happening to the minor, and with respect to the other portion of the property, the inclination of the father, even after he was dead, had the greatest weight, and that, now that the minor is dead, gives the property to his own heirs."

The question to be decided is, "Whether it was one property?" And then, if they employ this argument by way of invalidating the other, "That there can be many heirs of one property for quite dissimilar causes," the question to be decided arises out of that argument, namely "Whether there can be more heirs than one, of different classes and character, to one property?"

XXII. Therefore, in one statement of the case, it has been understood how there are more reasons than one, more topics than one to invalidate such reasons, and besides that, more questions than one for the decision of the judge. Now let us look to the rules for this class of question. We must consider in what the rights of each party, or of all the parties (if there are many parties to the suit), consist. The beginning, then, appears derived from nature; but some things seem to have become adopted in practice for some consideration of expediency which is either more or less evident to us. But afterwards things which were approved of, or which seemed useful, either through habit, or because of their truth, appeared to have been confirmed by laws, and some things seem to be a law of nature, which it is not any vague opinion, but a sort of innate instinct that implants in us, as religion, piety, revenge for injuries, gratitude, attention to superiors, and truth. They call religion, that which is conversant with the fear of, and ceremonious observance paid to the gods; they call that piety, which warns us to fulfil our duties towards our country, our parents, or others connected with us by ties of blood, gratitude is that which retains a recollection of honours and benefits conferred on one, and acts of friendship done to one, and which shows itself by a requital of good offices, revenge for injuries is that by which we repel violence and insult from ourselves and from those who ought to be dear to us, by defending or avenging ourselves, and by means of which we punish offences, attention to superiors, they call the feeling under the influence of which we feel reverence for and pay respect to those who excel us in wisdom or honour or in any dignity, truth, they style that habit by which we take care that nothing has been or shall be done in any other manner than what we state. And the laws of nature themselves are less inquired into in a controversy of this sort, because they have no particular connexion with the civil law of which we are speaking and also, because they are somewhat remote from ordinary understandings. Still it is often desirable to introduce them for the purpose of some comparison, or with a view to add dignity to the discussion.

But the laws of habit are considered to be those which without any written law, antiquity has sanctioned by the common consent of all men. And with reference to this habit there are some laws which are now quite fixed by their antiquity. Of which sort there are many other laws also, and among them far the greatest part of those laws which the praetors are in the habit of including in their edicts. But some kinds of law have already been established by certain custom, such as those relating to covenants, equity, formal decisions. A covenant is that which is agreed upon between two parties, because it is considered to be so just that it is said to be enforced by justice, equity is that which is equal to all men, a formal decision is that by which something has been established by the declared opinion of some person or persons authorized to pronounce one. As for regular laws, they can only be ascertained from the laws. It is desirable, then, by trying over every part of the law, to take notice of and to extract from these portions of the law whatever shall appear to arise out of the case itself, or out of a similar one, or out of one of greater or less importance. But since, as has been already said, there are two kinds of common topics, one of which contains the amplification of a doubtful matter, and the other of a certain one, we must consider what the case itself suggests, and what can be and ought to be amplified by a common topic. For certain topics to suit every possible case cannot be laid down, and perhaps in most of them it will be necessary at times to rely on the authority of the lawyers, and at times to speak against it. But we must consider, in this case and in all cases, whether the case itself suggests any common topics besides those which we have mentioned.

Now let us consider the juridical kind of inquiry and its different divisions.

XXIII. The juridical inquiry is that in which the nature of justice and injustice, and the principle of reward or punishment, is examined. Its divisions are two, one of which we call the absolute inquiry, and the other the one which is accessory. That is the absolute inquiry which itself contains in itself the question of right and not right, not as the inquiry about facts does, in an overhand and obscure manner, but openly and intelligibly. It is of this sort.—When the Thebans had defeated the Lacedaemonians in war, as it was nearly universal custom among the Greeks, when they were waging war against one another, for those who were victorious to erect some trophy on their borders, for the sake only of declaring their victory at present, not that it might remain for ever as a memorial of the war, they erected a brazen trophy. They are accused before the Amphictyons, that is, before the common council of Greece. The charge is, "They ought not to have done so." The denial is, "We ought." The question is, "Whether they ought." The reason is, "For we gained such glory by our valour in that war, that we wished to leave an everlasting memorial of it to posterity." The argument adduced to invalidate this is, "But still it is not right for Greeks to erect an eternal memorial of then enmity to Greeks." The question to be decided is, "As for the sake of celebrating their own excessive valour Greeks have erected an imperishable monument of their enmity to Greeks, whether they have done well or ill?" We, therefore, have now put this reason in the mouth of the Thebans, in order that this class of cause which we are now considering might be thoroughly understood. For if we had furnished them with that argument which is perhaps the one which they actually used, "We did so because our enemies warred against us without any considerations of justice and piety," we should then be digressing to the subject of retorting an accusation, of which we will speak hereafter. But it is manifest that both kinds of question are incidental to this controversy. And arguments must be derived for it from the same topics as those which are applicable to the cause depending on matters of fact, which has been all ready treated of. But to take many weighty common topics both from the cause itself, if there is any opportunity for employing the language of indignation or complaint, and also from the advantage and general character of the law, will be not only allowable, but proper, if the dignity of the cause appears to require such expedients.

XXIV. At present let us consider the assumptive portion of the juridical inquiry. But it is then called assumptive, when the fact cannot be proved by its own intrinsic evidence, but is defended by some argument brought from extraneous circumstances. Its divisions are four in number: comparison, the retort of the accusation, the refutation of it as far as regards oneself, and concession.

Comparison is when any action which intrinsically cannot be approved, is defended by reference to that for the sake of which it was done. It is something of this sort:—"A certain general, when he was blockaded by the enemy and could not escape by any possible means, made a covenant with them to leave behind his arms and his baggage, on condition of being allowed to lead away his soldiers in safety. And he did so. Having lost his arms and his baggage, he saved his men, beyond the hopes of any one. He is prosecuted for treason." Then comes the definition of treason. But let us consider the topic which we are at present discussing.

The charge is, "He had no business to leave behind the arms and baggage." The denial is, "Yes, he had." The question is, "Whether he had any right to do so?" The reason for doing so is, "For else he would have lost all his soldiers." The argument brought to invalidate this is either the conjectural one, "They would not have been lost," or the other conjectural one, "That was not your reason for doing so." And from this arise the questions for decision: "Whether they would have been lost?" and, "Whether that was the reason why he did so?" Or else, this comparative reason which we want at this minute: "But it was better to lose his soldiers than to surrender the arms and baggage to the enemy." And from this arises the question for the decision of the judges: "As all the soldiers must have been lost unless they had come into this covenant, whether it was better to lose the soldiers, or to agree to these conditions?"

It will be proper to deal with this kind of cause by reference to these topics, and to employ the principles of, and rules for the other statements of cases also. And especially to employ conjectures for the purpose of invalidating that which those who are accused will compare with the act which is alleged against them as a crime. And that will be done if either that result which the advocates for the defence say would have happened unless that action had been performed which is now brought before the court, be denied to have been likely to ensue; or if it can be proved that it was done with a different object and in a different manner from that stated by the man who is on his trial. The confirmation of that statement, and also the argument used by the opposite party to invalidate it, must both be derived from the conjectural statement of the case. But if the accused person is brought before the court, because of his action coming under the name of some particular crime, (as is the case in this instance, for the man is prosecuted for treason), it will be desirable to employ a definition and the rules for a definition.

XXV. And this usually takes place in this kind of examination, so that it is desirable to employ both conjecture and definition. But if any other kind of inquiry arises, it will be allowable on similar principles to transfer to it the rules for that kind of inquiry. For the accuser must of all things take pains to invalidate, by as many reasons as possible, the very fact on account of which the person on his trial thinks that it is granted to him that he was right. And it is easy to do so, if he attempts to overturn that argument by as many statements of the case as he can employ.

But comparison itself, when separated from the other kinds of discussion, will be considered according to its own intrinsic power, if that which is mentioned in the comparison is shown, either not to have been honourable, or not to have been useful, or not to have been necessary, or not so greatly useful, or not so very honourable, or not so exceedingly necessary.

In the next place it is desirable for the accuser to separate the action which he himself is accusing, from that which the advocate for the defence compares with it. And he will do that if he shows that it is not usually done in such a manner, and that it ought not to be done so, and that there is no reason why this thing should be done on this account; for instance, that those things which have been provided for the sake of safety, should be surrendered to the enemy for the sake of safety. Afterwards it will be desirable to compare the injury with the benefit, and altogether to compare the action which is impeached with that which is praised by the advocate for the defence or which is attempted to be proved as what must inevitably have ensued, and then, by disparaging the one at the same time to exaggerate the importance of the mischief caused by the other. That will be effected if it be shown that that which the person on his trial avoided was more honourable, more advantageous, and more necessary than that which he did. But the influence and character of what is honourable, and useful, and necessary, will be ascertained in the rules given for deliberation.

In the next place, it will be desirable to explain that comparative kind of judicial decision as if it were a deliberative cause and then afterwards to discuss it by the light thrown on it by rules for deliberation. For let this be the question for judicial decision which we have already mentioned—"As all the soldiers would have been lost if they had not come to this agreement, was it better for the soldiers to be lost, or to come to this agreement?" It will be desirable that this should be dealt with with reference to the topics concerning deliberation, as if the matter were to come to some consultation.

XXVI. But the advocate for the defence will take the topics in accordance with which other statements of the case are made by the accuser, and will prepare his own defence from those topics with reference to the same statements. But all other topics which belong to the comparison, he will deal with in the contrary manner.

The common topics will be these,—the accuser will press his charges against the man who confesses some discreditable or pernicious action, or both, but still seeks to make some defence, and will allege the mischievous or discreditable nature of his conduct with great indignation. The advocate for the defence will insist upon it, that no action ought to be considered pernicious or discreditable, or, on the other hand, advantageous or creditable, unless it is ascertained with what intention, at what time, and on what account it was done. And this topic is so common, that if it is well handled in this cause it is likely to be of great weight in convincing the hearers. And there is another topic, by means of which the magnitude of the service done is demonstrated with very great amplification, by reference to the usefulness, or honourableness, or necessity of the action. And there is a third topic, by means of which the matter which is expressed in words is placed before the eyes of those men who are the hearers, so that they think that they themselves also would have done the same things, if the same circumstances and the same cause for doing so had happened to them at the same time.

The retorting of a charge takes place, when the accused person, having confessed that of which he is accused, says that he did it justifiably, being induced by the sin committed against him by the other party. As in this case—"Horatius, when he had slain the three Curiatii and lost his two brothers, returned home victorious. He saw his sister not troubled about the death of her brothers, but at the same time calling on the name of Curiatius, who had been betrothed to her, with groans and lamentation. Being indignant, he slew the maid". He is prosecuted.

The charge is, "You slew your sister wrongfully". The refutation is "I slew her lawfully". The question is, "Whether he slew her lawfully". The reason is, "Yes, for she was lamenting the death of enemies, and was indifferent to that of her brothers, she was grieved that I and the Roman people were victorious". The argument to invalidate this reason is, "Still she ought not to have been put to death by her brother without being convicted". On this the question for the decision of the judges is, "Whether when Horatia was showing her indifference to the death of her brothers, and lamenting that of the enemy, and not rejoicing at the victory of her brother and of the Roman people, she deserved to be put to death by her brother without being condemned".

XXVII For this kind of cause, in the first place, whatever is given out of the other statements of cases ought to be taken, as has been already enjoined when speaking of comparison. After that, if there is any opportunity of doing so, some statement of the case ought to be employed by which he to whom the crime is imputed may be defended. In the next place, we ought to argue that the fault which the accused person is imputing to another, is a lighter one than that which he himself committed; in the next place, we ought to employ some portion of a demurrer, and to show by whom, and through whose agency, and how, and when that matter ought to have been tried, or adjudged, or decided. And at the same time, we ought to show that it was not proper that punishment should have been inflicted before any judgment was pronounced. Then we must also point out the laws and the course of judicial proceeding by which that offence which the accused person punished of his own accord, might have been chastised according to precedent, and by the regular course of justice. In the next place, it will be right to deny that it is proper to listen to the charge which is brought by the accused person against his victim, when he who brings it did not choose to submit it to the decision of the judges, and it may be urged that one ought to consider that on which no decision has been pronounced, as if it had not been done, and after that to point out the impudence of those men who are now before the judges accusing the man whom they themselves condemned without consulting the judges, and are now bringing him to trial on whom they have already inflicted punishment. After this we may say that it is bringing irregularity into the courts of justice, and that the judges will be advancing further than their power authorizes them, if they pronounce judgment at the same time in the case of the accused person, and of him whom the accused person impeaches. And in the next place, we may point out if this rule is established, and if men avenge one offence by another offence, and one injury by another injury, what vast inconvenience will ensue from such conduct, and that if the person who is now the prosecutor had chosen to do so too, there would have been no need of this trial at all, and that if every one else were to do so, there would be an end of all courts of justice.

After that it may be pointed out, that even if the maiden who is now accused by him of this crime had been convicted, he would not himself have had any right to inflict punishment on her, so that it is a shameful thing that the man who would have had no right to punish her, even if she had been convicted, should have punished her without her being even brought to trial at all. And then the accused person may be called upon to produce the law which he says justifies his having acted in such a manner.

After that, as we have enjoined when speaking of comparison, that that which is mentioned in comparison should be disparaged by the accuser as much as possible, so, too, in this kind of argument, it will be advantageous to compare the fault of the party on whom the accusation is retorted with the crime of the accused person who justified his action as having been lawfully done. And after that it is necessary to point out that that is not an action of such a sort, that on account of it this other crime ought to have been committed. The last point, as in the case of comparison, is the assumption of a judicial decision, and the dilating upon it in the way of amplification, in accordance with the rules given respecting deliberation.

XXVIII But the advocate for the defence will invalidate what is urged by means of other statements from those topics which have already been given. But the demurrer itself he will prove first of all, by dwelling on the guilt and audacity of the man to whom he imputes the crime, and by bringing it before the eyes of the judges with as much indignation as possible if the case admits of it, and also with vehement complaint, and afterwards by proving that the accused person chastised the offence more lightly than the offender deserved, by comparing the punishment inflicted with the injury done. In the next place, it will be desirable to invalidate by opposite arguments those topics which are handled by the prosecutor in such a way that they are capable of being refuted and retorted, of which kind are the three last topics which I have mentioned. But that most vehement attack of the prosecutors, by which they attempt to prove that irregularity will be introduced into all the courts of justice if power is given to any man of inflicting punishment on a person who has not been convicted, will have its force much weakened, first of all, if the injury be shown to be such as appears intolerable not only to a good man but absolutely to any freeman, and in the next place to be so manifest that it could not have been denied even by the person who had done it, and moreover, of such a kind that the person who did chastise it was the person who above all others was bound to chastise it. So that it was not so proper nor so honourable for that matter to be brought before a court of justice as for it to be chastised in that manner in which, and by that person by whom it was chastised, and lastly, that the case was so notorious that there was no occasion whatever for a judicial investigation into it. And here it will be proper to show, by arguments and by other similar means, that there are very many things so atrocious and so notorious, that it is not only not necessary, but that it is not even desirable to wait for the slow proceedings of a judicial trial.

There is a common topic for an accuser to employ against a person, who, when he cannot deny the fact of which he is accused, still derives some hope from his attempt to show that irregularity will be introduced into all courts of justice by such proceedings. And here there will come in the demonstration of the usefulness of judicial proceedings, and the complaint of the misfortune of that person who has been punished without being condemned; and the indignation to be expressed against the audacity and cruelty of the man who has inflicted the punishment. There is also a topic for the advocate for the defence to employ, in complaining of the audacity of the person whom he chastised; and in urging that the case ought to be judged of, not by the name of the action itself, but with reference to the intention of the person who committed it, and the cause for which, and the time at which it was committed. And in pointing out what great mischief will ensue either from the injurious conduct, or the wickedness of some one, unless such excessive and undisguised audacity were chastised by him whose reputation, or parents, or children, or something else which either necessarily is, or at least ought to be dear to every one, is affected, by such conduct.

XXIX. The transference of an accusation takes place when the accusation of that crime which is imputed to one by the opposite party is transferred to some other person or circumstance. And that is done in two ways. For sometimes the motive itself is transferred, and sometimes the act. We may employ this as an instance of the transference of the motive:—"The Rhodians sent some men as ambassadors to Athens. The quaestors did not give the ambassadors the money for their expenses which they ought to have given them. The ambassadors consequently did not go. They are impeached." The charge brought against them is, "They ought to have gone." The denial is, "They ought not." The question is, "Whether they ought." The reason alleged is, "Because the money for their expenses, which is usually given to ambassadors from the public treasury, was not given to them by the quaestor." The argument brought to invalidate that reason is, "Still you ought to have discharged the duty which was entrusted to you by the public authority." The question for the decision of the judges is, "Whether, as the money which ought to have been supplied from the public treasury was not furnished to those men who were appointed ambassadors, they were nevertheless bound to discharge the duties of their embassy." In this class of inquiry, as in all the other kinds, it will be desirable to see if anything can be assumed, either from a conjectural statement of the case, or from any other kind of statement. And after that, many arguments can be brought to bear on this question, both from comparison, and from the transference of the guilt to other parties.

But the prosecutor will, in the first place, if he can, defend the man through whose fault the accused person says that that action was done; and if he cannot, he will declare that the fault of the other party has nothing to do with this trial, but only the fault of this man whom he himself is accusing. Afterwards he will say that it is proper for every one to consider only what is his own duty; and that if the one party did wrong, that was no reason for the other doing wrong too. And in the next place, that if the other man has committed a fault, he ought to be accused separately as this man is, and that the accusation of the one is not to be mixed up with the defence of the other.

But when the advocate for the defence has dealt with the other arguments, if any arise out of other statements of the case, he will argue in this way with reference to the transference of the charge to other parties. In the first place, he will point out to whose fault it was owing that the thing happened; and in the next place, as it happened in consequence of the fault of some one else, he will point out that he either could not or ought not to have done what the prosecutor says he ought: that he could not, will be considered with reference to the particulars of expediency, in which the force of necessity is involved; that he ought not, with reference to the honourableness of the proceeding. We will consider each part more minutely when talking of the deliberative kind of argument. Then he will say, that everything was done by the accused person which depended on his own power; that less was done than ought to have been, was the consequence of the fault of another person. After that, in pointing out the criminality of that other person, it will be requisite to show how great the good will and zeal of the accused person himself was. And that must be established by proofs of this sort—by his diligence in all the rest of the affair, by his previous actions, or by his previous expressions. And it may be well to show that it would have been advantageous to the man himself to have done this, and disadvantageous not to have done it, and that to have done it would have been more in accordance with the rest of his life, than the not having done it, which, was owing to the fault of the other party.

XXX But if the criminality is not to be transferred to some particular person, but to some circumstance, as in this very case—"If the quaestor had been dead, and on that account the money had not been given to the ambassadors," then, as the accusation of the other party, and the denial of the fault is removed, it will be desirable to employ the other topics in a similar manner, and to assume whatever is suitable to one's purpose from the divisions of admitted facts. But common topics are usually nearly the same to both parties, and then, after the previous topics are taken for granted, will suit either to the greatest certainty. The accuser will use the topic of indignation at the fact, the defender, when the guilt belongs to another and does not attach to himself, will urge that he does not deserve to have any punishment inflicted on him.

But the removal of the criminality from oneself is effected when the accused person declares, that what is attributed to him as a crime did not affect him or his duty, and asserts that if there was any criminality in it, it ought not to be attributed to him. That kind of dispute is of this sort—"In the treaty which was formerly made with the Samnites, a certain young man of noble birth held the pig which was to be sacrificed, by the command of the general. But when the treaty was disavowed by the senate, and the general surrendered to the Samnites, one of the senators asserted that the man who held the pig ought also to be given up." The charge is, "He ought to be given up." The denial is, "He ought not." The question is, "Whether he ought or not." The reason is, "For it was no particular duty of mine, nor did it depend on my power, being as young as I was, and only a private individual, and while the general was present with the supreme authority and command, to take care that the treaty was solemnised with all the regular formalities." The argument to invalidate this reason is, "But since you became an accomplice in a most infamous treaty, sanctioned with the most formal solemnities of religion, you ought to be surrendered." The question for the judges to decide is "Whether, since a man who had no official authority was present, by the command of the general, aiding and abetting in the adopting of the treaty, and in that important religious ceremony, he ought to be surrendered to the enemy or not." This kind of question is so far different from the previous one, because in that the accused person admits that he ought to have done what the prosecutor says ought to have been done, but he attributes the cause to some particular circumstance or person, which was a hindrance to his own intention, without having recourse to any admission. For that has greater force, which will be understood presently. But in this case a man ought not to accuse the opposite party, nor to attempt to transfer the criminality to another, but he ought to show that that has not and never has had any reference whatever to himself, either in respect of power or duty. And in this kind of cause there is this new circumstance, that the prosecutor often works up a fresh accusation out of the topics employed, to remove the guilt from the accused person. As for instance,—"If any one accuses a man who, while he was praetor, summoned the people to take up arms for an expedition, at a time when the consuls were in the city." For as in the previous instance the accused person showed that the matter in question had no connexion with his duty or his power, so in this case also, the prosecutor himself, by removing the action done from the duty and power of the person who is put on his trial, confirms the accusation by this very argument. And in this case it will be proper for each party to examine, by means of all the divisions of honour and expediency, by examples, and tokens, and by arguing what is the duty, or right, or power of each individual, and whether he had that right, and duty, and power which is the subject of the present discussion, or not. But it will be desirable for common topics to be assumed from the case itself, if there is any room in it for expressions of indignation or complaint.

XXXI. The admission of the fact takes place, when the accused person does not justify the fact itself, but demands to be pardoned for it. And the parts of this division of the case are two: purgation and deprecation. Purgation is that by which (not the action, but) the intention of the person who is accused, is defended. That has three subdivisions,—ignorance, accident, necessity.

Ignorance is when the person who is accused declares that he did not know something or other. As, "There was a law in a certain nation that no one should sacrifice a calf to Diana. Some sailors, when in a terrible tempest they were being tossed about in the open sea, made a vow that if they reached the harbour which they were in sight of, they would sacrifice a calf to the god who presided over that place. Being ignorant of the law, when they landed, they sacrificed a calf." They are prosecuted. The accusation is, "You sacrificed a calf to a god to whom it was unlawful to sacrifice a calf." The denial consists in the admission which has been already stated. The reason is, "I was not aware that it was unlawful." The argument brought to invalidate that reason is, "Nevertheless, since you have done what was not lawful, you are according to the law deserving of punishment." The question for the decision of the judge is, "Whether, as he did what he ought not to have done, and was not aware that he ought not to have done so, he is worthy of punishment or not."

But accident is introduced into the admission when it is proved that some power of fortune interfered with his intention; as in this case:—"There was a law among the Lacedaemonians, that if the contractor failed to supply victims for a certain sacrifice, he should be accounted guilty of a capital offence; and accordingly, the man who had contracted to supply them, when the day of the sacrifice was at hand, began to drive in cattle from the country into the city. It happened on a sudden that the river Eurotus, which flows by Lacedaemon, was raised by some violent storms, and became so great and furious that the victims could not by any possibility be conveyed across. The contractor, for the sake of showing his own willingness, placed all the victims on the bank of the river, in order that every one on the other side of the river might be able to see them. But though, everyone was aware that it was the unexpected rise of the river which hindered him from giving effect to his zeal, still some people prosecuted him on the capital charge." The charge was, "The victims which you were bound to furnish for the sacrifice were not furnished." The reply was an admission of the fact. The reason alleged was, "For the river rose on a sudden, and on that account it was impossible to convey them across." The argument used to invalidate that reason was, "Nevertheless, since what the law enjoins was not done, you are deserving of punishment." The question for the decision of the judges was, "Whether, as in that respect the contractor did not comply with the law, being prevented by the unexpected rise of the river which hindered his giving effect to his zeal, he is deserving of punishment."

XXXII. But the plea of necessity is introduced when the accused person is defended as having done what he is accused of having done under the influence of compulsion. In this way:—"There is a law among the Rhodians, that if any vessel with a beak is caught in their harbour, it shall be confiscated. There was a violent storm at sea; the violence of the winds compelled a vessel, against the will of her crew, to take refuge in the harbour of the Rhodians. On this the quaestor claims the vessel for the people. The captain of the ship declared that it was not just that it should be confiscated." The charge is, "A ship with a beak was caught in the harbour." The reply is an admission of the fact. The reason given is, "We were driven into the harbour by violence and necessity." The argument brought to invalidate that reason is, "Nevertheless, according to the law that ship ought to become the property of the people." The question for the decision of the judge is, "Whether, as the law confiscates every ship with a beak which is found in the harbour, and as this ship, in spite of the endeavours of her crew, was driven into the harbour by the violence of the tempest, it ought to be confiscated."

We have collected these examples of these three kinds of cases into one place, because a similar rule for the arguments required for these prevails in all of them. For in all of them, in the first place, it is desirable, if the case itself affords any opportunity of doing so, that a conjecture should be introduced by the accuser, in order that that which it will be stated was not done intentionally, may be demonstrated by some suspicious circumstances, to have been done intentionally. In the next place, it will be well to introduce a definition of necessity, or of accident, or of ignorance, and to add instances to that definition, in which ignorance, or accident, or necessity appear to have operated, and to distinguish between such instances and the allegations put forward by the accused person, (that is to say, to show that there is no resemblance between them,) because this was a lighter or an easier matter, or one which did not admit of any one's being ignorant respecting it, or one which gave no room for accident or necessity. After that it must be shown that it might have been avoided, and, that the accused person might have prevented it if he had done this thing, or that thing, or that he might have guarded against being forced to act in such a manner. And it is desirable to prove by definitions that this conduct of his ought not to be called imprudence, or accident, or necessity, but indolence, indifference, or fatuity.

And if any necessity alleged appears to have in it anything discreditable, it will be desirable for the opponent, by a chain of common topics, to prove that it would have been better to suffer anything, or even to die, rather than to submit to a necessity of the sort. And then, from these topics, which have been already discussed when we spoke of the question of fact, it will be desirable to inquire into the nature of law and equity, and, as if we were dealing with an absolute juridical question, to consider this point by itself separately from all other points. And in this place, if there should be an opportunity, it will be desirable to employ instances in which there can be no room for any similar excuse, and also to institute a comparison, showing that there would have been more reason to allow it in them, and by reference to the divisions of deliberation, it may be shown that it is admitted that that action which was committed by the adversary is confessed to have been discreditable and useless, that it is a matter of great importance, and one likely to cause great mischief, if such conduct is overlooked by those who have authority to punish it.

XXXIII. But the advocate for the defence will be able to convert all these arguments, and then to use them for his own purposes. And he will especially dwell on the defence of his intentions, and in exaggerating the importance of that which was an obstacle to his intentions, and he will show that he could not have done more than he did do, and he will urge that in all things the will of the doer ought to be regarded, and that it is quite impossible that he should be justly convicted of not being free from guilt, and that under his name the common powerlessness of mankind is sought to be convicted. Then, too, he will say that nothing can be more scandalous than for a man who is free from guilt, not also to be free from punishment. But the common topics for the prosecutor to employ are these, one resting on the confession of the accused person, and the other pointing out what great licence for the violation of the law will follow, if it is once laid down that the thing to be inquired into is not the action but the cause of the action. The common topics for the advocate for the defence to employ are, a complaint of that calamity which has taken place by no fault of his, but in consequence of some overruling power, and a complaint also of the power of fortune and the powerless state of men, and an entreaty that the judges should consider his intentions, and not the result. And in the employment of all these topics it will be desirable that there should be inserted a complaint of his own unhappy condition, and indignation at the cruelty of his adversaries.

And no one ought to marvel, if in these or other instances he sees a dispute concerning the letter of the law added to the rest of the discussion. And we shall have hereafter to speak of this subject separately, because some kinds of causes will have to be considered by themselves, and with reference to their own independent merits, and some connect with themselves some other kind of question also. Wherefore, when everything is cleared up, it will not be difficult to transfer to each cause whatever is suitable to that particular kind of inquiry, as in all these instances of admission of the fact, there is involved that dispute as to the law, which is called the question as to the letter and spirit of the law. But as we were speaking of the admission of the fact we gave rules for it. But in another place we will discuss the letter and the spirit of the law. At present we will limit our consideration to the other division of the admission of the fact.

XXXIV. Deprecation is when it is not attempted to defend the action in question, but entreaties to be pardoned are employed. This kind of topic can hardly be approved of in a court of justice, because, when the offence is admitted, it is difficult to prevail on the man who is bound to be the chastiser of offences to pardon it. So that it is allowable to employ that kind of address only when you do not rest the whole cause on it. As for instance, if you were speaking in behalf of some illustrious or gallant man, who has done great services to the republic, you might, without appearing to have recourse to deprecation, still employ it in this manner:—"But if, O judges, this man, in return for the services which he has done you, and the zeal which he has displayed in your cause at all times, were now, when he himself is in such peril, to entreat you, in consideration of his many good actions, to pardon this one error, it would only be what is due both to your own character for clemency, and to his virtue, O judges, for you to grant him this indulgence at his request." Then it will be allowable to dwell upon the services which he has done, and by the use of some common topic to lead the judges to feel an inclination to pardon him.

Wherefore, although this kind of address has no proper place in judicial proceedings, except to a certain limited extent; still, because both the portion which is allowable must be employed at times, and because it is often to be employed in all its force in the senate or in the council, we will give rules for it also. For there was a long deliberation in the senate and in the council about Syphax; and there was a long discussion before Lucius Opimius and his bench of assessors respecting Quintus Numitorius Pullus; and in this case the entreaty for pardon had more influence than the strict inquiry into the case. For he did not find it so easy to prove that he had always been well affected towards the Roman people, by employing the statement of the case founded on conjecture, as to show that it was reasonable to pardon him on account of his subsequent services, when he added the topics of deprecation to the rest of his defence.

XXXV. It will be desirable, therefore, for the man who entreats to be pardoned for what he admits that he has done, to enumerate whatever services of his he is able to, and, if possible, to show that they are greater than those offences which he has committed, so that it may appear that more good than evil has proceeded from him; and then to put forward also the services done by his ancestors, if there are any such; and also to show that he did what he did, not out of hatred, or out of cruelty, but either through folly, or owing to the instigation of some one, or for some other honourable or probable cause; and after that to promise and undertake that he has been taught by this error of his, and confirmed in his resolution also by the kindness of those who pardon him, to avoid all such conduct in future. And besides this, he may hold out a hope that he will hereafter be able, in some respect or other, to be of great use to those who pardon him now; he will find it serviceable to point out that he is either related to the judges, or that he has been as far back as possible an hereditary friend of theirs; and to express to them the earnestness of his good-will towards them, and the nobility of the blood and dignity of those men who are anxious for his safety. And all other qualities and circumstances which, when attributable to persons, confer honour and dignity on them, he, using no complaint, and avoiding all arrogance, will point out as existing in himself, so that he may appear to deserve some honour rather than any kind of punishment; and after that it will be wise of him to mention other men who have been pardoned for greater offences.

And he will do himself a great deal of good if he shows that he himself, when in power, was merciful and inclined to pardon others. And the offence of which he is now accused must be extenuated and made to appear as trifling as possible; and it must be shown to be discreditable, or at all events inexpedient, to punish such a man as he is. After that it will be advisable to seek to move pity by use of common topics, according to those rules which have been laid down in the first book.

XXXVI. But the adversary will exaggerate the offences; he will say that nothing was done ignorantly, but that everything was the result of deliberate wickedness and cruelty. He will show that the accused person has been pitiless, arrogant, and (if he possibly can) at all times disaffected, and that he cannot by any possibility be rendered friendly. If he mentions any services done by him, he will prove that they were done for some private object, and not out of any good will; or else he will prove that he has conceived hatred since or else that all those services have been effaced by his frequent offences, or else that his services are of less importance than his injuries, or that, as he has already received adequate honours for his services, he ought also to have punishment inflicted on him for the injuries which he has committed. In the next place, he will urge that it is discreditable or pernicious that he should be pardoned. And besides that, it will be the very extremity of folly not to avail oneself of one's power over a man, over whom one has often wished to have power, and that it is proper to consider what feelings, or rather what hatred they ought to entertain towards him. But one common topic to be employed will be indignation at his offence, and another will be the argument, that it is right to pity those who are in distress, owing to misfortune, and not those who are in such a plight through their own wickedness.

Since, then, we have been dwelling so long on the general statement of the case, on account of the great number of its divisions, in order to prevent any one's mind from being so distracted by the variety and dissimilarity of circumstances, and so led into some errors, it appears right also to remind the reader of what remains to be mentioned of that division of the subject, and why it remains. We have said, that that was the juridical sort of examination in which the nature of right and wrong, and the principles of reward and punishment, were investigated. We have explained the causes in which inquiry into right and wrong is proceeded with. It remains now to explain the principles which regulate the distribution of rewards and punishments.

XXXVII. For there are many causes which consist of a demand of some reward. For there is often question before the judges of the rewards to be conferred on prosecutors, and very often some reward is claimed for them from the senate, or from the bench of judges. And it is not advisable that any one should think that, when we are adducing some instance which is under discussion in the senate, we by so doing are abandoning the class of judicial examples. For whatever is said with reference to approving or disapproving of a person, when the consideration of the opinions of the judges is adapted to that form of expression, that, even although it is treated with reference to the language in which the opinion is couched, is a deliberative argument, still, because it has especial reference to some person, it is to be accounted also judicial. And altogether, a man who has diligently investigated the meaning and nature of all causes will perceive that they differ both in character and in form; but in the other divisions he will see them all consistent with each other, and every one connected with the other. At present, let us consider the question of rewards. Lucius Licinius Crassus, the consul, pursued and destroyed a band of people in the province of the Nearer Gaul, who were collected together under no known or regular leader, and who had no name or number of sufficient importance to be entitled enemies of the Roman people; but still they made the province unsafe by their constant sallies and piratical outbreaks. He returns to Rome. He demands a triumph. Here, as also in the case of the employment of deprecation, it does not at all concern us to supply reasons to establish and to invalidate such a claim, and so to come before the judges; because, unless some other statement of the case is also put forth, or some portion of such statement, the matter for the decision of the judges will be a simple one, and will be contained in the question itself. In the case of the employment of deprecation, in this manner: "Whether so and so ought to be punished." In this instance, in such a manner: "Whether he ought to be rewarded."

Now we will furnish some topics suitable for the investigation into the principles of rewards.

XXXVIII. The principle, then, on which rewards are conferred is distributable into four divisions: as to the services done; the person who has done them; the kind of reward which is to be conferred; and the means of conferring it. The services done will be considered with reference to their own intrinsic merits, and to the time, and to the disposition of the man who did them, and to their attendant circumstances. They will be examined with reference to their own intrinsic merits, in this manner:—Whether they are important or unimportant; whether they were difficult or easy; whether they are of a common or extraordinary nature; whether they are considered honourable on true or false principles. And with reference to the time at which they were done:—If they were done at a time when we had need of them; when other men could or would not help them; if they were done when all other hope had failed. With reference to the disposition of the man who did them:—If he did not do them with a view to any advantage of his own, but if he did everything else for the express purpose of being able to do this afterwards. And with reference to the attendant circumstances:—If what was done appears not to have been done by chance, but in consequence of some deliberate design, or if chance appears to have hindered the design.

But, with respect to the man who did the service in question, it will be requisite to consider in what manner he has lived, and what expense or labour he has devoted to that object; whether he has at any time done any other similar action; whether he is claiming a reward for himself for what is in reality the result of another person's exertions, or of the kindness of the gods. Whether he has ever, in the case of any one else, pronounced that he ought not to be rewarded for such a reason; or, whether he has already had sufficient honour paid to him for what he has done; or, whether what has been done is an action of such a sort that, if he had not done it, he would have been deserving of punishment; but that he does not deserve reward for having done it; or, whether he is premature in his demand for a reward, and is proposing to sell an uncertain hope for a certain reward; or, whether he claims the reward in order to avoid some punishment, by its appearing as if the case had already been decided in his favour.

XXXIX. But as to the question of the reward, it will be necessary to consider what reward, how great a reward is claimed, and why it is claimed; and also, to what reward, and to how great a reward, the conduct in question is entitled. And in the next place, it will be requisite to inquire what men had such honours paid them in the time of our ancestors, and for what causes those honours were paid. And, in the next place, it will be urged that they ought not to be made too common. And this will be one common topic for any one who speaks in opposition to a person who claims a reward;—that rewards for virtue and eminent services ought to be considered serious and holy things, and that they ought not to be conferred on worthless men, or to be made common by being bestowed on men of no particular eminence. And another will be, to urge that men will become less eager to practise virtue when the reward of virtue has been made common; for those things which are scarce and difficult of attainment appear honourable and acceptable to men. And a third topic is, to put the question, whether, if there are any instances of men who, in the times of our ancestors, were thought worthy of such honours on account of their eminent virtue, they will not be likely to think it some diminution of their own glory, when they see that such men as these have such rewards conferred on them. And then comes the enumeration of those men, and the comparison of them with those against whom the orator is speaking. But the topics to be used by the man who is claiming the reward are, first of all, the exaggeration of his own action; and next, the comparison of the actions of those men who have had rewards conferred on them with his own; and lastly, he will urge that other men will be repelled from the pursuit of virtue if he himself is denied the reward to which he is entitled.

But the means of conferring the rewards are taken into consideration when any pecuniary reward is asked for; for then it is necessary to consider whether there is an abundance of land, and revenue, and money, or a dearth of them. The common topics are,—that it is desirable to increase the resources of the state, not to diminish them; and that he is a shameless man who is not content with gratitude in requital of his services, but who demands also solid rewards. But, on the other hand, it may be urged, that it is a sordid thing to argue about money, when the question is about showing gratitude to a benefactor; and that the claimant is not asking wages for a piece of work, but honour such as is due for an important service.

And we have now said enough about the statements of cases; now it seems necessary to speak of those controversies which turn upon the letter of the law.

XL. The controversy turns upon the letter of the law when some doubt arises from the consideration of the exact terms in which it is drawn up. That arises from ambiguity, from the letter of the law, from its intention, from contrary laws, from ratiocination, and definition. But a controversy arises from ambiguity, when it is an obscure point what was the intention of the writer, because the written words mean two or even more different things. In this manner:—"The father of a family, when he was making his son his heir, left a hundredweight of silver plate to his wife, in these terms: "Let my heir give my wife a hundredweight of silver plate, consisting of such vessels as may be chosen. After he was dead, the mother demands of her son some very magnificent vessels of very valuable carving. He says that he is only bound to give her those vessels which he himself chooses." Here, in the first place, it is necessary to show if possible that the will has not been drawn up in ambiguous terms, because all men in ordinary conversation are accustomed to employ that expression, whether consisting of one word or more, in that meaning in which the speaker hopes to show that this is to be understood. Then it is desirable to prove that from both the preceding and subsequent language of the will, the real meaning which is being sought may be made evident. So that if all the words, or most of them, were considered separately by themselves, they would appear of doubtful meaning. But as for those which can be made intelligible by a consideration of the whole document, these have no business to be thought obscure.

In the next place, it will be proper to draw one's conclusion as to the intentions which were entertained by the writer from all his other writings, and actions, and sayings, and his general disposition, and from the usual tenor of his life; and to scrutinise that very document in which this ambiguous phrase is contained which is the subject of the present inquiry, all over, in all its parts, so as to see whether there is anything opposite to that interpretation which we contend for, or contrary to that which the adversary insists on adopting. For it will be easy to consider what it is probable that the man who drew up the document intended, from its whole tenor, and from the character of the writer, and from those other circumstances which are characteristic of the persons concerned. In the next place, it will be desirable to show, if the facts of the case itself afford any opportunity for doing so, that that meaning which the opposite party contends for, is a much more inconvenient one to adopt than that which we have assumed to be the proper one, because there is no possible means of carrying out or complying with that other meaning; but what we contend for can be accomplished with great ease and convenience.

As in this law (for there is no objection to citing an imaginary one for the sake of giving an instance, in order to the more easy comprehension of the matter):—"Let not a prostitute have a golden crown. If such a case exists, it must be confiscated." Now, in opposition to a man who contended that that was to become public property in accordance with this law, it might be argued, "that there could be no way of making a prostitute public property, and there is no intelligible meaning for the law if that is what is to be adopted as its proper construction; but as to the confiscation of anything made of gold, the management and the result is easy, and there is no difficulty in it."

XLI. And it will be desirable also to pay diligent attention to this point, whether if that sense is sanctioned which the opposite party contends for, any more advantageous, or honourable, or necessary object appears to have been omitted by the framer of the document in question. That will be done if we can prove that the object which we are attempting to prove is either honourable, or expedient, or necessary; and if we can also assert that the interpretation which our adversaries insist upon, is not at all entitled to such a character. In the next place, if there is in the law itself any controversy arising from any ambiguity, it will be requisite to take great care to show that the meaning which our adversaries adopt is provided for in some other law. But it will be very serviceable indeed to point out how the testator would have expressed himself, if he had wished the interpretation which the adversary puts upon his words to be carried into execution or understood. As for instance, in this cause, the one, I mean, in which the question is about the silver plate, the woman might argue, "That there was no use in adding the words 'as may be chosen,' if the matter was left to the selection of the heir; for if no such words had been inserted, there could have been no doubt at all that the heir might have given whatever he himself chose. So that it was downright madness, if he wished to take precautions in favour of his heir, to add words which might have been wholly left out without such omission prejudicing his heir's welfare."

Wherefore, it will be exceedingly advisable to employ this species of argument in such causes:—"If he had written with this intention he would not have employed that word; he would not have placed that word in that place;" for it is from such particulars as these that it is easiest to collect the intention of the writer. In the next place, it is necessary to inquire when the document was drawn up, in order that it may be understood what it was likely that he should have wished at such a time. Afterwards it will be advisable to point out, by reference to the topics furnished by the deliberative argument, what is more useful and what more honourable to the testator to write, and to the adversary to prove; and it will be well for both parties to employ common topics, if there is any room for extending either argument.

XLII. A controversy arises with respect to the letter of the document and to its meaning, when one party employs the very words which are set down in the paper; and the other applies all his arguments to that which he affirms that the framer of the document intended. But the intention of the framer of the document must be proved by the man who defends himself, by reference to that intention, to have always the same object in view and the same meaning; and it must also, either by reference to the action or to some result, be adapted to the time which the inquiry concerns. It must be proved always to have the same object in view, in this way:—"The head of a house, at a time when he had no children, but had a wife, inserted this clause in his will: 'If I have a son or sons born to me, he or they is or are to be my heir or heirs.' Then follow the ordinary provisions. After that comes the following clause: 'If my son dies before he comes into the property, which is held in trust for him, then,' says the clause, 'you shall be my reversionary heir.' He never has a son. His next of kin raise a dispute with the man who is named as the heir, in the case of the testator's son dying before he comes into the property which his guardians are holding for him." In this case it cannot be said that the meaning of the testator ought to be made to suit the time or some particular result, because that intention alone is proved on which the man who is arguing against the language of the will relies, in order to defend his own right to the inheritance.

There is another class of topics which introduce the question as to the meaning of expressions, in which the mere simple intention of the framer is not endeavoured to be proved, for that has the same weight with reference to every period and every action; but it is argued that it ought to be interpreted with reference to some particular action, or to some event happening at that particular time. And that is especially supported by the divisions of the juridical assumptive mode of investigation. For then the comparison is instituted; as in the case of "a man who, though the law forbad the gates to be opened by night, did open them in a certain war, and admitted some reinforcements into the town, in order to prevent their being overwhelmed by the enemy if they remained outside the gates; because the enemy were encamped close to the walls." Then comes the retorting of the charge; as in the case of "that soldier who, when the common law of all men forbad any one to kill a man, slew his own military tribune who was attempting to offer violence to him." Then comes the exculpation; as in the case of "that man who, when the law had appointed some particular days within which he was to proceed on his embassy, did not set out because the quaestor did not furnish him with money for his expenses." Then comes the admission of the fact by way of purgation, and also by the excuse of ignorance; as "in the case of the sacrificing a calf;" and with reference to compulsion, as "in the case of the beaked ship;" and with reference to accident, as "in the case of the sudden rise of the river Eurotas." Wherefore, it is best that the meaning should be introduced in such a way, as that the framer of the law should be proved to have intended some one definite thing; else in such a way that he should be proved to have meant this particular thing, under these circumstances, and at this time.

XLIII. He, therefore, who is defending the exact language of the law, will generally be able to use all these topics; and will always be able to use the greater part of them. First of all, he will employ a panegyric of the framer of it, and the common topic that those who are the judges have no business to consider anything except what is expressly stated in the law; and so much the more if any legal document be brought forward, that is to say, either the law itself, or some portion of the law. Afterwards—and this is a point of the greatest importance—he will employ a comparison of the action or of the charge brought by the opposite party with the actual words of the law; he will show what is contained in the law, what has been done, what the judge has sworn. And it will be well to vary this topic in many ways, sometimes professing to wonder in his own mind what can be said against this argument; sometimes recurring to the duty of the judge, and asking of him what more he can think it requisite to hear, or what further he expects; sometimes by bringing forward the adversary himself, as if in the position of a person making an accusation; that is to say, by asking him whether he denies that the law is drawn up in that manner, or whether he denies that he himself has contravened it, or disputed it. If he denies either of these points, then one must avow that one will say no more; if he denies neither of them, and yet continues to urge his arguments in opposition to one, then one must say that it is impossible for any one ever to expect to see a more impudent man. And it will be well to dwell on this point as if nothing besides were to be said, as if nothing could be said in contradiction, by reciting several times over what is written; by often contrasting the conduct of the adversary with what is written; and sometimes by recurring vehemently to the topic of the judge himself; in which one will remind the judge of what oath he has taken, of what his conduct is bound to be; and urge that there are two causes on account of which a judge is bound to hesitate, one if the law be obscurely worded, the other if the adversary denies anything. But as in this instance the wording of the law is plain, and the adversary admits every fact that is alleged, the judge has now nothing to do but to fulfil the law, and not to interpret it.

XLIV. When this point has been sufficiently insisted on, then it will be advisable to do away with the effect of those things which the adversary has been able to urge by way of objection. But such objections will be made if the framer of the law can be absolutely proved to have meant one thing, and written another; as in that dispute concerning the will which we mentioned just now: or some adventitious cause may be alleged why it was not possible or not desirable to obey the written law minutely. If it is stated that the framer of the law meant one thing, and wrote another, then he who appeals to the letter of the law will say that it is our business not to discuss the intention of a man who has left us a plain proof of that intention, to prevent our having any doubt about it; and that many inconveniences must ensue if the principle is laid down that we may depart from the letter of the law. For that then those who frame laws will not think that the laws which they are making will remain firm; and those who are judges will have no certain principle to follow if once they get into the habit of departing from the letter of the law. But if the intention of the framer of the law is what is to be looked at, then it is he, and not his adversaries, who relies on the meaning of the lawgiver. For that that person comes much nearer to the intention of the framer of a law who interprets it from his own writings, than he who does not look at the meaning of the framer of the law by that writing of his own which he has left to be as it were an image of his meaning, but who investigates it under the guidance of some private suspicions of his own.

If the party who stands on the meaning of the lawgiver brings forward any reasons, then, in the first place, it will be necessary to reply to those reasons; to urge how absurd it is for a man not to deny that he has acted contrary to the law, but at the same time to give some reason for having acted so. Then one will say too that all things are turned upside down; that formerly prosecutors were in the habit of trying to persuade the judges that the person who was being prosecuted before them was implicated in some fault, and of alleging some reasons which had instigated him to commit this fault; but that now the accused person himself is giving the reasons why he has offended against the laws. Then it will be proper to introduce this division, each portion of which will have many lines of argument suitable to it: in the first place, that there is no law with reference to which it is allowable to allege any reasons contrary to the law; in the next place, that if such a course is admissible in any law, this is such a law that it is not admissible with respect to it; and lastly, that, even if such reasons ever might be alleged, at all events this is not such a reason.

XLV. The first part of the argument is confirmed by pretty nearly the same topics as these: that the framer of the law was not deficient in either ability, or pains, or any faculty requisite to enable him to express plainly what his intention was; that it would not have been either displeasing or difficult to him to insert such an exception as that which the opposite party contends for in his law, if he thought any exception requisite; and in fact, that those people who frame laws often do insert clauses of exceptions. After that it is well to enumerate some of the laws which have exceptional clauses attached to them, and to take especial care to see whether in the law itself which is under discussion there is any exception made in any chapter, or whether the same man who framed this law has made exceptions in other laws, so that it may be more naturally inferred that he would have made exceptions in this one, if he had thought exceptions requisite; and it will be well also to show that to admit of a reason for violating the law is the same thing as abrogating the law, because when once such a reason is taken into consideration it is no use to consider it with reference to the law, inasmuch as it is not stated in the law. And if such a principle is once laid down, then a reason for violating the law, and a licence to do so, is given to every one, as soon as they perceive that you as judges decide the matter in a way which depends on the ability of the man who has violated the law, and not with reference to the law which you have sworn to administer. Then, too, one must point out that all principles on which judges are to judge, and citizens are to live, will be thrown into confusion if the laws are once departed from; for the judges will not have any rules to follow, if they depart from what is set down in the law, and no principles on which they can reprove others for having acted in defiance of the law. And that all the rest of the citizens will be ignorant what they are to do, if each of them regulates all his actions according to his own ideas, and to whatever whim or fancy comes into his head, and not according to the common statute law of the state.

After that it will be suitable to ask the judges why they occupy themselves at all with the business of other people;—why they allow themselves to be harassed in discharging the offices of the republic, when they might often spend the time in promoting their own ends and private interests;—why they take an oath in a certain form;—why they assemble at a regular time and go away at a regular time;—why no one of them ever alleges any reason for being less frequent in his discharge of his duty to the republic, except such as is set down in some formal law as an exception. And one may ask, whether they think it right that they should be bound down and exposed to so much inconvenience by the laws, and at the same time allow our adversaries to disregard the laws. After that it will be natural to put the question to the judges whether, when the party accused himself endeavours to set down in the law, as an exception, that particular case in which he admits that he has violated the law, they will consent to it. And to ask also, whether what he has actually done is more scandalous and more shameless than the exception which he wishes to insert in the law;—what indeed can be more shameless? Even if the judges were inclined to make such an addition to the law, would the people permit it? One might also press upon them that this is even a more scandalous measure, when they are unable to make an alteration in the language and letter of the law, to alter it in the actual facts, and to give a decision contrary to it; and besides, that it is a scandalous thing that anything should be taken from the law, or that the law should be abrogated or changed in any part whatever, without the people having any opportunity of knowing, or approving, or disapproving of what is done; that such conduct is calculated to bring the judges themselves into great odium; that it is not the proper time nor opportunity for amending the laws; that this ought only to be brought forward in an assembly of the people, and only to be done by the people; that if they now do so, the speaker would like to know who is the maker of the new law, and who are to obey it; that he sees actions impending, and wishes to prevent them; that as all such proceedings as these are exceedingly useless and abundantly discreditable, the law, whatever it is like, ought, while it exists, to be maintained by the judges, and hereafter, if it is disapproved of, to be amended by the people. Besides this, if there were no written law, we should take great trouble to find one; and we should not place any confidence in that man, not even if he were in no personal danger himself; but now, when there is a written law, it is downright insanity to attend to what that man says who has violated the law, rather than to the language of the law itself. By these and similar arguments it is proved that it is not right to admit any excuse which is contrary to the letter of the law.

XLVI. The second part is that in which it is desirable to prove that if such a proceeding is right with respect to other laws, it is not advisable with respect to this one. This will be shown if the law appears to refer to matters of the greatest importance, and usefulness, and honourableness, and sanctity; so that it is disadvantageous, or discreditable, or impious not to obey the law as carefully as possible in such a matter. Or the law may be proved to have been drawn up so carefully, and such great diligence may be shown to have been exercised in framing each separate provision of it, and in making every exception that was allowable, that it is not at all probable that anything proper to be inserted has been omitted in so carefully considered a document.

The third topic is one exceedingly necessary for a man who is arguing in defence of the letter of the law; by which it may be urged, that even if it is decent for an excuse to be admitted contrary to the letter of the law, still that excuse which is alleged by his adversaries is of all others the least proper to be so alleged. And this topic is necessary for him on this account,—because the man who is arguing against the letter of the law ought always to have some point of equity to allege on his side. For it is the greatest possible impudence for a man who wishes to establish some point in opposition to the exact letter of the law, not to attempt to fortify himself in so doing, with the assistance of the law. If therefore the accuser in any respect weakens the defence by this topic, he will appear in every respect to have more justice and probability in favour of his accusation. For all the former part of his speech has had this object,—that the judges should feel it impossible, even if they wished it, to avoid condemning the accused person; but this part has for its object the making them wish to give such a decision, even if it were not inevitable.

And that result will be obtained, if we use those topics by which guilt may be proved not to be in the man who defends himself, by using the topic of comparison, or by getting rid of the accusation, or by recrimination, or by some species of confession, (concerning all which topics we have already written with all the precision of which we were capable,) and if we take those which the case will admit of for the purpose of throwing discredit on the argument of our adversary;—or if reasons and arguments are adduced to show why or with what design those expressions were inserted in the law or will in question, so that our side of the question may appear established by the meaning and intention of the writer, and not only by the language which he has employed. Or the fact may be proved by other statements and arguments.

XLVII. But any one who speaks against the letter of the law will first of all introduce that topic by which the equity of the excuse is proved; or he will point out with what feelings, with what design, and on what account he did the action in question. And whatever excuse he alleges he will defend according to some of the rules which I have already given with respect to assumptions. And when he has dwelt on this topic for some time, and set forth the principles of his conduct and the equity of his cause in the most specious manner he can, he will also add, in opposition to the arguments of his adversaries, that it is from these topics for the most part that excuses which are admissible ought to be drawn. He will urge that there is no law which sanctions the doing of any disadvantageous or unjust action; that all punishments which are enacted by the laws have been enacted for the sake of chastising guilt and wickedness; that the very framer of the laws, if he were alive, would approve of this conduct, and would have done the very same thing himself if he had been in similar circumstances. And that it is on this account that the framer of the law appointed judges of a certain rank and age, in order that there might be men, not capable merely of reading out what he had written, which any boy might do, but able also to understand his thoughts and to interpret his intentions. He will add, that that framer of the law, if he had been intrusting the laws which he was drawing up to foolish men and illiterate judges, would have set down everything with the most scrupulous diligence; but, as it is, because he was aware what sort of men were to be the judges, he did not put down many things which appeared to him to be evident; and he expected that you would be not mere readers of his writings, but interpreters of his intentions. Afterwards he will proceed to ask his adversaries—"What would you say if I had done so and so?" "What would you think if so and so had happened?" "Suppose any one of those things had happened which would have had a most unfailing excuse, or a most undeniable necessity, would you then have prosecuted me?" But the law has nowhere made any such exception. It follows, therefore, that it is not every possible circumstance which is mentioned in the written law but that some things which are self-evident are guarded against by unexpressed exceptions.

Then he will urge, that nothing could be carried on properly either by the laws or by any written document whatever, or even in daily conversation, or in the commands given in a private household, if every one chose to keep his eyes on the exact language of the order, and not to take into consideration the intentions of him who uttered the order.

XLVIII. After that he will be able, by reference to the divisions of usefulness and honour, to point out how inexpedient or how dishonourable that would have been which the opposite party say ought to have been done, or to be done now. And on the other hand, how expedient and how honourable that is which we have done, or demand should be done. In the next place, he will urge that we set a value on our laws not on account of their wording, which is a slight and often obscure indication of their intention, but on account of the usefulness of those things concerning which they are written, and the wisdom and diligence of those men who wrote them. Afterwards he will proceed to describe what the law is, so that it shall appear to consist of meanings, not of words; and that the judge may appear to be obedient to the law, who follows its meaning and not its strict words. After that he will urge how scandalous it is that he should have the same punishment inflicted on him who has violated the law out of some mere wickedness and audacity, as on the man who, on account of some honourable or unavoidable reason, has departed not from the spirit of the law, but from its letter. And by these and similar arguments he will endeavour to prove that the excuse is admissible, and is admissible in this law, and that the excuse which he himself is alleging ought to be admitted.

And, as we said that this would be exceedingly useful to the man who was relying on the letter of the law, to detract in some degree from that equity which appeared to be on the side of the adversary; so also it will be of the greatest advantage to the man who is speaking in opposition to the letter of the law, to convert something of the exact letter of the law to his own side of the argument, or else to show that something has been expressed ambiguously. And afterwards, to take that portion of the doubtful expression which may serve his own purpose, and defend it; or else to introduce some definition of a word, and to bring over the meaning of that word which seems unfavourable to him to the advantage of his own cause, or else, from what is set down in the law to introduce something which is not set down by means of ratiocination, which we will speak of presently. But in whatever matter, however little probable it may be, he defends himself by an appeal to the exact letter of the law, even when his case is full of equity, he will unavoidably gain a great advantage, because if he can withdraw from the cause of the opposite party that point on which it principally relies, he will mitigate and take off the effect of all its violence and energy. But all the rest of the common topics taken from the divisions of assumptive argument will suit each side of the question. It will also be suitable for him whose argument takes its stand on the letter of the law, to urge that laws ought to be looked at, not with reference to the advantage of that man who has violated them, but according to their own intrinsic value, and that nothing ought to be considered more precious than the laws. On the other side, the speaker will urge, that laws depend upon the intention of the framer of them, and upon the general advantage, not upon words, and also, how scandalous it is for equity to be overwhelmed by a heap of letters, and defended in vain by the intention of the man who drew up the law.

XLIX. But from contrary laws a controversy arises, when two or more laws appear to be at variance with one another In this manner—There is a law, "That he who has slain a tyrant shall receive the regard of men who conquer at Olympia, and shall also ask whatever he pleases of the magistrate, and the magistrate shall grant it to him." There is also another law—"When a tyrant is slain, the magistrate shall also put to death his five nearest relations." Alexander, who was the tyrant of Pheræ, a city in Thessaly, was slain by his own wife, whose name was Thebe, at night, when he was in bed with her, she, as a reward, demands the liberty of her son whom she had by the tyrant. Some say that according to this law that son ought to be put to death. The matter is referred to a court of justice. Now in a case of this kind the same topics and the same rules will suit each side of the question, because each party is bound to establish his own law, and to invalidate the one contrary to it. First of all, therefore, it is requisite to show the nature of the laws, by considering which law has reference to more important, that is to say, to more honourable and more necessary matters. From which it results, that if two or more, or ever so many laws cannot all be maintained, because they are at variance with one another, that one ought to be considered the most desirable to be maintained, which appears to have reference to the most important matters. Then comes the question also, which law was passed last; for the newest law is the most important. And also, which law enjoins anything, and which merely allows it; for that which is enjoined is necessary, that which is allowed is optional. Also one must consider by which law a penalty is appointed for the violation of it; or which has the heaviest penalty attached to it; for that law must be the most carefully maintained which is sanctioned by the most severe penalties. Again, one must inquire which law enjoins, and which forbids anything; for it often happens that the law which forbids something appears by some exception as it were to amend the law which commands something. Then, too, it is right to consider which law comprehends the entire class of subjects to which it refers, and which embraces only a part of the question; which may be applied generally to many classes of questions, and which appears to have been framed to apply to some special subject. For that which has been drawn up with reference to some particular division of a subject, or for some special purpose, appears to come nearer to the subject under discussion, and to have more immediate connexion with the present action. Then arises the question, which is the thing which according to the law must be done immediately; which will admit of some delay or slackness in the execution. For it is right that that should be done first which must be done immediately. In the next place, it is well to take pains that the law one is advocating shall appear to depend on its own precise language; and that the law with a contrary sense should appear to be introduced with a doubtful interpretation, or by some ratiocination or definition, in order that that law which is expressed in plain language may appear to be the more solemn and efficient. After that it will be well to add the meaning of the law which is on one's own side according to the strict letter of it; and also to explain the opposite law so as to make it appear to have another meaning, in order that, if possible, they may not seem to be inconsistent with one another. And, last of all, it will be a good thing, if the cause shall afford any opportunity for so doing, to take care that on our principles both the laws may seem to be upheld, but that on the principle contended for by our adversaries one of them must be put aside. It will be well also to consider all the common topics and those which the cause itself furnishes, and to take them from the most highly esteemed divisions of the subjects of expediency and honour, showing by means of amplification which law it is most desirable to adhere to.

L. From ratiocination there arises a controversy when, from what is written somewhere or other, one arrives at what is not written anywhere; in this way:—"If a man is mad, let those of his family and his next of kin have the regulation of himself and of his property." And there is another law—"In whatever manner a head of a family has made his will respecting his family and his property, so let it be." And another law—"If a head of a family dies intestate, his family and property shall belong to his relations and to his next of kin." A certain man was convicted of having murdered his father. Immediately, because he was not able to escape, wooden shoes were put upon his feet, and his mouth was covered with a leathern bag, and bound fast, then he was led away to prison, that he might remain there while a bag was got ready for him to be put into and thrown into a river. In the meantime some of his friends bring tablets to the prison, and introduce witnesses also; they put down those men as his heirs whom he himself desires; the will is sealed; the man is afterwards executed. There is a dispute between those who are set down as his heirs in the will, and his next of kin, about his inheritance. In this instance there is no positive law alleged which takes away the power of making a will from people who are in such a situation. But from other laws, both those which inflict a punishment of this character on a man guilty of such a crime, and those, too, which relate to a man's power of making a will, it is possible to come by means of ratiocination to a conclusion of this sort, that it is proper to inquire whether he had the power of making a will.

But we think that these and such as these are the common topics suitable to an argument of this description. In the first place, a panegyric upon, and a confirmation of that writing which you are producing. Then a comparison of the matter which is the subject of discussion, with that which is a settled case, in such a manner that the case which is under investigation may appear to resemble that about which there are settled and notorious rules. After that, one will express admiration, (by way of comparison), how it can happen that a man who admits that this is fair, can deny that other thing, which is either more equitable still, or which rests on exactly similar principles; then, too, one will contend that the reason why there is no precise law drawn up for such a case, is because, as there was one in existence applicable to the other case, the framer of that law thought that no one could possibly entertain a doubt in this case; and afterwards it will be well to urge that there are many cases not provided for in many laws, which beyond all question were passed over merely because the rule as to them could be so easily collected out of the other cases which were provided for; and last of all, it is necessary to point out what the equity of the case requires, as is done in a plain judicial case.

But the speaker who is arguing on the other side is bound to try and invalidate the comparison instituted, which he will do if he can show that that which is compared is different from that with which it is compared in kind, in nature, in effect, in importance, in time, in situation, in character, in the opinion entertained of it; if it is shown also in what class that which is adduced by way of comparison ought to stand, and in what rank that also ought to be considered, for the sake of which the other thing is mentioned. After that, it will be well to point out how one case differs from the other, so that it does not seem that any one ought to have the same opinion of both of them. And if he himself also is able to have recourse to ratiocination, he must use the same ratiocination which has been already spoken of. If he cannot, then he will declare that it is not proper to consider anything except what is written; that all laws are put in danger if comparisons are once allowed to be instituted; that there is hardly anything which does not seem somewhat like something else; that when there are many circumstances wholly dissimilar, still there are separate laws for each individual case; and that all things can be proved to be like or unlike to each other. The common topics derived from ratiocination ought to arrive by conjecture from that which is written to that which is not written; and one may urge that no one can embrace every imaginable case in a written law, but that he frames a law best who takes care to make one thing understood from another. One may urge, too, that in opposition to a ratiocination of this sort, conjecture is no better than a divination, and that it would be a sign of a very stupid framer of laws not to be able to provide for everything which he wished to.

LI. Definition is when a word is set down in a written document, whose exact meaning is inquired into, in this manner:—There is a law, "Whoever in a severe tempest desert their ship shall be deprived of all their property; the ship and the cargo shall belong to those men who remain by the ship." Two men, when they were sailing on the open sea, and when the ship belonged to one of them and the cargo to another, noticed a shipwrecked man swimming and holding out his hands to them. Being moved with pity they directed the ship towards him, and took the man into their vessel. A little afterwards the storm began to toss them also about very violently, to such a degree that the owner of the ship, who was also the pilot, got into a little boat, and from that he guided the ship as well as he could by the rope by which the boat was fastened to the ship, and so towed along; but the man to whom the cargo belonged threw himself on his sword in despair. On this the shipwrecked man took the helm and assisted the ship as far as he could. But after the waves went down and the tempest abated, the ship arrived in harbour. But the man who had fallen on his sword turned out to be but slightly wounded, and easily recovered of his wound. And then every one of these three men claimed the ship and cargo for his own. Every one of them relies on the letter of the law to support their claim, and a dispute arises as to the meaning of the words. For they seek to ascertain by definitions what is the meaning of the expressions "to abandon the ship," "to stand by the ship," and even what "the ship" itself is. And the question must be dealt with with reference to all the same topics as are employed in a statement of the case which turns upon a definition.

Now, having explained all those argumentations which are adapted to the judicial class of causes, we will proceed in regular order to give topics and rules for the deliberative and demonstrative class of arguments; not that there is any cause which is not at all times conversant with some statement of the case or other; but because there are nevertheless some topics peculiar to these causes, not separated from the statement of the case, but adapted to the objects which are more especially kept in view by these kinds of argumentation.

For it seems desirable that in the judicial kind the proper end is equity; that is to say, some division of honesty. But in the deliberative kind Aristotle thinks that the proper object is expediency; we ourselves, that it is expediency and honesty combined. In the demonstrative kind it is honesty only. Wherefore, in this kind of cause also, some kinds of argumentation will be handled in a common manner, and in similar ways to one another. Some will be discussed more separately with reference to their object, which is what we must always keep in view in every kind of speech. And we should have no objection to give an example of each kind of statement of the case, if we did not see that, as obscure things are made more plain by speaking of them, so also things which are plain are sometimes made more obscure by a speech. At present let us go on to precepts of deliberation.

LII. Of matters to be aimed at there are three classes; and on the other hand there is a corresponding number of things to be avoided. For there is something which of its own intrinsic force draws us to itself, not catching us by any idea of emolument, but alluring us by its own dignity. Of this class are virtue, science, truth. And there is something else which seems desirable, not on account of its own excellence or nature, but on account of its advantage and of the utility to be derived from it—such as money. There are also some things formed of parts of these others in combination, which allure us and draw us after them by their own intrinsic character and dignity, and which also hold out some prospect of advantage to us, to induce us to seek it more eagerly, as friendship, and a fair reputation; and from these their opposites will easily be perceived, without our saying anything about them.

But in order that the principle may be explained in the more simple way, the rules which we have laid down shall be enumerated briefly. For those which belong to the first kind of discussion are called honourable things; those which belong to the second, are called useful things; but this third thing, because it contains some portion of what is honourable, and because the power of what is honourable is the more important part, is perceived to be altogether a compound kind, made up of a twofold division; still it derives its name from its better part, and is called honourable. From this it follows, that there are these parts in things which are desirable,—what is honourable, and what is useful. And these parts in things which are to be avoided,—what is dishonourable, and what is useless. Now to these two things there are two other important circumstances to be added,—necessity and affection: the one of which is considered with reference to force, the other with reference to circumstances and persons. Hereafter we will write more explicitly about each separately. At present we will explain first the principles of what is honourable.

LIII. That which either wholly or in some considerable portion of it is sought for its own sake, we call honourable: and as there are two divisions of it, one of which is simple and the other twofold, let us consider the simple one first. In that kind, then, virtue has embraced all things under one meaning and one name; for virtue is a habit of the mind, consistent with nature, and moderation, and reason. Wherefore, when we have become acquainted with all its divisions, it will be proper to consider the whole force of simple honesty.

It has then four divisions—prudence, justice, fortitude, and temperance. Prudence is the knowledge of things which are good, or bad, or neither good nor bad. Its parts are memory, intelligence, and foresight. Memory is that faculty by which the mind recovers the knowledge of things which have been. Intelligence is that by which it perceives what exists at present. Foresight is that by which anything is seen to be about to happen, before it does happen. Justice is a habit of the mind which attributes its proper dignity to everything, preserving a due regard to the general welfare. Its first principles proceed from nature. Subsequently some practices became established by universal custom, from a consideration of their utility; afterwards the fear of the laws and religion sanctioned proceedings which originated in nature, and had been approved of by custom.

Natural law is that which has not had its origin in the opinions of men, but has been implanted by some innate instinct, like religion, affection, gratitude, revenge, attention to one's superiors, truth. Religion is that which causes men to pay attention to, and to respect with fixed ceremonies, a certain superior nature which men call divine nature. Affection is that feeling under the influence of which kindness and careful attention is paid to those who are united to us by ties of blood, or who are devoted to the service of their country. Gratitude is that feeling in which the recollection of friendship, and of the services which we have received from another, and the inclination to requite those services, is contained. Revenge is that disposition by which violence and injury, and altogether everything which can be any injury to us, is repelled by defending oneself from it, or by avenging it. Attention is that feeling by which men obey when they think those who are eminent for worth or dignity, worthy of some special respect and honour. Truth is that by which those things which are, or which have been previously, or which are about to happen, are spoken of without any alteration.

LIV. Conventional law is a principle which has either derived its origin in a slight degree from nature, and then has been strengthened by habit, like religion; or, if we see any one of those things which we have already mentioned as proceeding from nature strengthened by habit; or, if there is anything to which antiquity has given the force of custom with the approbation of everybody: such as covenants, equity, cases already decided. A covenant is that which is agreed upon between two parties; equity is that which is equally just for every one; a case previously decided is one which has been settled by the authoritative decision of some person or persons entitled to pronounce it.

Legal right is that which is contained in that written form which is delivered to the people to be observed by them.

Fortitude is a deliberate encountering of danger and enduring of labour. Its parts are magnificence, confidence, patience, and perseverance. Magnificence is the consideration and management of important and sublime matters with a certain wide-seeing and splendid determination of mind. Confidence is that feeling by which the mind embarks in great and honourable courses with a sure hope and trust in itself. Patience is a voluntary and sustained endurance, for the sake of what is honourable or advantageous, of difficult and painful labours. Perseverance is a steady and lasting persistence in a well-considered principle.

Temperance is the form and well-regulated dominion of reason over lust and other improper affections of the mind. Its parts are continence, clemency, and modesty.

Continence is that by which cupidity is kept down under the superior influence of wisdom. Clemency is that by which the violence of the mind, when causelessly excited to entertain hatred against some one else, is restrained by courtesy. Modesty is that feeling by which honourable shame acquires a valuable and lasting authority. And all these things are to be sought for themselves, even if no advantage is to be acquired by them. And it neither concerns our present purpose to prove this, nor is it agreeable to our object of being concise in laying down our rules.

But the things which are to be avoided for their own sake, are not those only which are the opposites to these; as indolence is to courage, and injustice to justice; but those also which appear to be near to and related to them, but which, in reality, are very far removed from them. As, for instance, diffidence is the opposite to confidence, and is therefore a vice; audacity is not the opposite of confidence, but is near it and akin to it, and, nevertheless, is also a vice. And in this manner there will be found a vice akin to every virtue, and either already known by some particular name—as audacity, which is akin to confidence; pertinacity, which is bordering on perseverance; superstition, which is very near religion,—or in some cases it has no fixed name. And all these things, as being the opposites of what is good, we class among things to be avoided. And enough has now been said respecting that class of honourable things which is sought in every part of it for itself alone.

LV. At present it appears desirable to speak of that in which advantage is combined with honour, and which still we style simply honourable. There are many things, then, which allure us both by their dignity and also by the advantage which may be derived from them: such as glory, dignity, influence, friendship. Glory is the fact of a person's being repeatedly spoken of to his praise; dignity is the honourable authority of a person, combined with attention and honour and worthy respect paid to him. Influence is a great abundance of power or majesty, or of any sort of resource. Friendship is a desire to do service to any one for the sake of the person himself to whom one is attached, combined with a corresponding inclination on his part towards oneself. At present, because we are speaking of civil causes, we add the consideration of advantage to friendship, so that it appears a thing to be sought for the sake of the advantage also: wishing to prevent those men from blaming us who think that we are including every kind of friendship in our definition.

But although there are some people who think that friendship is only to be desired on account of the advantage to be derived from it; some think it is to be desired for itself alone; and some, that it is to be desired both for its own sake and for the sake of the advantage to be derived from it. And which of these statements is the most true, there will be another time for considering. At present it may be laid down, as far as the orator is concerned, that friendship is a thing to be desired on both accounts. But the consideration of the different kinds of friendship, (since they are partly formed on religious considerations, and partly not; and because some friendships are old, and some new; and because some originated in kindness shown by our friends to us, and some in kindness shown by ourselves to them; and because some are more advantageous, and others less,) must have reference partly to the dignity of the causes in which it originates, partly to the occasion when it arises, and also to the services done, the religious motives entertained, and its antiquity.

LVI. But the advantages consist either in the thing itself, or in extraneous circumstances; of which, however, by far the greater portion is referable to personal advantage; as there are some things in the republic which, so to say, refer to the person of the state,—as lands, harbours, money, fleets, sailors, soldiery, allies; by all which things states preserve their safety and their liberty. There are other things also which make a thing more noble looking, and which still are less necessary; as the splendid decorating and enlarging of a city, or an extraordinary amount of wealth, or a great number of friendships and alliances. And the effect of all these things is not merely to make states safe and free from injury, but also noble and powerful. So that there appears to be two divisions of usefulness,—safety and power. Safety is the secure and unimpaired preservation of a sound state. Power is a possession of things suitable to preserving what is one's own, and to acquiring what belongs to another. And in all those things which have been already mentioned, it is proper to consider what is difficult to be done, and what can be done with ease. We call that a thing easy to be done, which can be done without great labour, or expense, or annoyance, or perhaps without any labour, expense, or annoyance at all, and in the shortest possible time. But that we call difficult to be done which, although it requires labour, expense, trouble and time, and has every possible characteristic of difficulty about it, or, at all events, the most numerous and most important ones, still, when these difficulties are encountered, can be completed and brought to an end.

Since, then, we have now discussed what is honourable and what is useful, it remains for us to say a little of those things which we have said are attached to these other things; namely, affection and necessity.

LVII. I think, then, that necessity means that which cannot be resisted by any power; that which cannot be softened nor altered. And that this may be made more plain, let us examine into the meaning of it by the light of examples, so as to see what its character and how great its power is. "It is necessary that anything made of wood must be capable of being burnt with fire. It is necessary that a mortal body should at some time or other die." And it is so necessary, that that power of necessity which we were just now describing requires it; which cannot by any force whatever be either resisted, or weakened, or altered. Necessities of this kind, when they occur in oratory, are properly called necessities; but if any difficult circumstances arise, then we shall consider in the previous examination whether it, the thing in question, be possible to be done. And it seems to me, that I perceive that there are some kinds of necessity which admit of additions, and some which are simple and perfect in themselves. For we say in very different senses:—"It is necessary for the people of Casilinum to surrender themselves to Hannibal;" and, "It is necessary that Casilinum should come into the power of Hannibal." In the one case, that is, in the first case, there is this addition to the proposition:—"Unless they prefer perishing by hunger." For if they prefer that, then it is not necessary for them to surrender. But in the latter proposition such an addition has no place; because whether the people of Casilinum choose to surrender, or prefer enduring hunger and perishing in that manner, still it is necessary that Casilinum must come into the power of Hannibal. What then can be effected by this division of necessity? I might almost say, a great deal, when the topic of necessity appears such as may be easily introduced. For when the necessity is a simple one, there will be no reason for our making long speeches, as we shall not be able by any means to weaken it; but when a thing is only necessary provided we wish to avoid or to obtain something, then it will be necessary to state what advantage or what honour is contained in that addition. For if you will take notice, while inquiring what this contributes to the advantage of the state, you will find that there is nothing which it is necessary to do, except for the sake of some cause which we call the adjunct. And, in like manner, you will find that there are many circumstances of necessity to which a similar addition cannot be made; of such sort are these:—"It is necessary that mortal men should die;" without any addition:—"It is not necessary for men to take food;" with this exception,—"Unless they have an objection to dying of hunger."

Therefore, as I said before, it will be always proper to take into consideration the character of that exception which is added to the original proposition. For it will at all times have this influence, that either the necessity must be explained with reference to what is honourable, in this manner:—"It is necessary, if we wish to live with honour;" or with reference to safety, in this manner:—"It is necessary, if we wish to be safe;" or with reference to convenience, in this manner:—"It is necessary, if we are desirous to live without annoyance."

LVIII. And the greatest necessity of all appears to be that which arises from what is honourable; the next to it is that which arises from considerations of safety; the third and least important is that which has ideas of convenience involved in it. But this last can never be put in comparison with the two former. But it is often indispensable to compare these together; so that although honour is more precious than safety, there is still room to deliberate which one is to consult in the greatest degree. And as to this point, it appears possible to give a settled rule which may be of lasting application. For in whatever circumstances it can happen by any possibility that while we are consulting our safety, that slight diminution of honesty which is caused by our conduct may be hereafter repaired by virtue and industry, then it seems proper to have a regard for our safety. But when that does not appear possible, then we must think of nothing but what is honourable. And so in a case of that sort when we appear to be consulting our safety, we shall be able to say with truth that we are also keeping our eyes fixed on what is honourable, since without safety we can never attain to that end. And in these circumstances it will be desirable to yield to another, or to put oneself in another's place, or to keep quiet at present and wait for another opportunity. But when we are considering convenience, it is necessary to consider this point also,—whether the cause, as far as it has reference to usefulness, appears of sufficient importance to justify us in taking anything from splendour or honour. And while speaking on this topic, that appears to me to be the main thing, that we should inquire what that is which, whether we are desirous of obtaining or avoiding it, is something necessary; that is to say, what is the character of the addition; in order that, according as the matter is found to be, so we may exert ourselves, and consider the most important circumstances as being also the most necessary.

Affection is a certain way of looking at circumstances either with reference to the time, or to the result, or management of affairs, or to the desires of men, so that they no longer appear to be such as they were considered previously, or as they are generally in the habit of being considered. "It appears a base thing to go over to the enemy; but not with the view which Ulysses had when he went over. And it is a useless act to throw money into the sea; but not with the design which Aristippus had when he did so." There are, therefore, some circumstances which may be estimated with reference to the time at which and the intention with which they are done; and not according to their own intrinsic nature. In all which cases we must consider what the times require, or what is worthy of the persons concerned; and we must not think merely what is done, but with what intention, with what companions, and at what time, it is done. And from these divisions of the subject, we think that topics ought to be taken for delivering one's opinion.

LIX. But praise and blame must be derived from those topics which can be employed with respect to persons, and which we have already discussed. But if any one wishes to consider them in a more separate manner, he may divide them into the intention, and the person of the doer, and extraneous circumstances. The virtue of the mind is that concerning the parts of which we have lately spoken; the virtues of the body are health, dignity, strength, swiftness. Extraneous circumstances are honour, money, relationship, family, friends, country, power, and other things which are understood to be of a similar kind. And in all these, that which is of universal validity ought to prevail here; and the opposites will be easily understood as to their description and character.

But in praising and blaming, it will be desirable to consider not so much the personal character of, or the extraneous circumstances affecting the person of whom one is speaking, as how he has availed himself of his advantages. For to praise his good fortune is folly, and to blame it is arrogance; but the praise of a man's natural disposition is honourable, and the blame of it is a serious thing.

Now, since the principles of argumentation in every kind of cause have been set forth, it appears that enough has been said about invention, which is the first and most important part of rhetoric. Wherefore, since one portion of my work has been brought down to its end from the former book; and since this book has already run to a great length, what remains shall be discussed in subsequent books.

[The two remaining books are lost.]

THE TREATISE OF M. T. CICERO ON TOPICS,

DEDICATED TO CAIUS TREBATIUS.

* * * * *

THE ARGUMENT.

This treatise was written a short time before the events which gave rise to the first Philippic. Cicero obtained an honorary lieutenancy, with the intention of visiting his son at Athens; on his way towards Rhegium he spent an evening at Velia with Trebatius, where he began this treatise, which he finished at sea, before he arrived in Greece. It is little more than an abstract of what had been written by Aristotle on the same subject, and which Trebatius had begged him to explain to him; and Middleton says, that as he had not Aristotle's essay with him, he drew this up from memory, and he appears to have finished it in a week, as it was the nineteenth of July that he was at Velia, and he sent this work to Trebatius from Rhegium on the twenty-seventh. He himself apologizes to Trebatius in the letter which accompanied it, (Ep. Fam. vii. 19,) for its obscurity, which however, he says, was unavoidably caused by the nature of the subject.

I. We had begun to write, O Caius Trebatius, on subjects more important and more worthy of these books, of which we have published a sufficient number in a short time, when your request recalled me from my course. For when you were with me in my Tusculan villa, and when each of us was separately in the library opening such books as were suited to our respective tastes and studies, you fell on a treatise of Aristotle's called the Topics; which he has explained in many books; and, excited by the title, you immediately asked me to explain to you the doctrines laid down in those books. And when I had explained them to you, and told you that the system for the discovery of arguments was contained in them, in order that we might arrive, without making any mistake, at the system on which they rested by the way discovered by Aristotle, you urged me, modestly indeed, as you do everything, but still in a way which let me plainly see your eagerness to be gratified, to make you master of the whole of Aristotle's method. And when I exhorted you, (not so much for the sake of saving myself trouble, as because I really thought it advantageous for you yourself,) either to read them yourself, or to get the whole system explained to you by some learned rhetorician, you told me that you had already tried both methods. But the obscurity of the subject deterred you from the books; and that illustrious rhetorician to whom you had applied answered you, I suppose, that he knew nothing of these rules of Aristotle. And this I was not so much surprised at, namely, that that philosopher was not known to the rhetorician, inasmuch as he is not much known even to philosophers, except to a very few.

And such ignorance is the less excusable in them, because they not only ought to have been allured by those things which he has discovered and explained, but also by the incredible richness and sweetness of his eloquence. I could not therefore remain any longer in your debt, since you often made me this request, and yet appeared to fear being troublesome to me, (for I could easily see that,) lest I should appear unjust to him who is the very interpreter of the law. In truth, as you had often written many things for me and mine, I was afraid that if I delayed obliging you in this, it would appear very ungrateful or very arrogant conduct on my part. But while we were together, you yourself are the best witness of how I was occupied; but after I left you, on my way into Greece, when neither the republic nor any friends were occupying my attention, and when I could not honourably remain amid the armies, (not even if I could have done so safely,) as soon as I came to Velia and beheld your house and your family, I was reminded of this debt; and would no longer be wanting to your silent request. Therefore, as I had no books with me, I have written these pages on my voyage, from memory; and I have sent them to you while on my journey, in order that by my diligence in obeying your commands, I might rouse you to a recollection of my affairs, although you do not require a reminder. But, however, it is time to come to the object which we have undertaken.

II. As every careful method of arguing has two divisions,—one of discovering, one of deciding,—Aristotle was, as it appears to me, the chief discoverer of each. But the Stoics also have devoted some pains to the latter, for they have diligently considered the methods of carrying on a discussion by that science which they call dialectics; but the art of discovering arguments, which is called topics, and which was more serviceable for practical use, and certainly prior in the order of nature, they have wholly disregarded. But we, since both parts are of the greatest utility, and since we intend to examine each if we have time, will now begin with that which is naturally the first.

As therefore the discovery of those things which are hidden is easy, if the place where they are hidden is pointed out and clearly marked; so, when we wish to examine any argument, we ought to know the topics,—for so they are called by Aristotle, being, as it were, seats from which arguments are derived. Therefore we may give as a definition, that a topic is the seat of an argument, and that an argument is a reason which causes men to believe a thing which would otherwise be doubtful. But of those topics in which arguments are contained, some dwell on that particular point which is the subject of discussion; some are derived from external circumstances. When derived from the subject itself, they proceed at times from it taken as a whole, at times from its parts, at times from some sign, and at others from things which are disposed in some manner or other towards the subject under discussion; but those topics are derived from external circumstances which are at a distance and far removed from the same subject.

But a definition is employed with reference to the entire matter under discussion which unfolds the matter which is the subject of inquiry as if it had been previously enveloped in mystery. The formula of that argument is of this sort: "Civil law is equity established among men who belong to the same city, for the purpose of insuring each man in the possession of his property and rights: and the knowledge of this equity is useful: therefore the knowledge of civil law is useful." Then comes the enumeration of the parts, which is dealt with in this manner: "If a slave has not been declared free either by the censor, or by the praetor's rod, or by the will of his master, he is not free: but none of those things is the case: therefore he is not free." Then comes the sign; when some argument is derived from the meaning of a word, in this way:—As the Ælian Sentian law orders an assiduus [3] to support an assiduus, it orders a rich man to support a rich man, for a rich man is an assiduus, called so, as Ælius says, from *asse dando*.

[3] "*Assiduus*. Prop, sitting down, seated, and so, well to do in the world, rich. The derivation *ab assis duendis* is therefore to be rejected. Servius Tullius divided the Roman people into two classes, *assidui, i. e.* the rich, who could sit down and take their ease, and *proletarii,* or *capite censi,* the poor."—Riddle, in voc. *Assiduus,* quoting this passage. One does not see, however, why Ælius and Cicero should not understand the meaning and derivation of a Latin word. Smith's Dict. Ant. takes no notice of the word at all.

III. Arguments are also derived from things which bear some kind of relation to that which is the object of discussion. But this kind is distributed under many heads; for we call some connected with one another either by nature, or by their form, or by their resemblance to one another, or by their differences, or by their contrariety to one another, or by adjuncts, or by their antecedents, or by their consequents, or by what is opposed to each of them, or by causes, or by effects, or by a comparison with what is greater, or equal, or less.

Arguments are said to be connected together which are derived from words of the same kind. But words are of the same kind which, originating from one word, are altered in various ways; as, "*sapiens, sapienter, sapientia*." The connexion of these words is called [Greek: *suxugia*]; from which arises an argument of this kind: "If the land is common, every one has a right to feed his cattle on it."

An argument is derived from the kind of word, thus: "Since all the money has been bequeathed to the woman, it is impossible that that ready money which was left in the house should not have been bequeathed. For the species is never separated from the genus as long as it retains its name: but ready money retains the name of money: therefore it is plain that it was bequeathed."

An argument is derived from the species, which we may sometimes name, in order that it may be more clearly understood; in this manner: "If the money was bequeathed to Fabia by her husband, on the supposition that she was the mother of his family; if she was not his wife, then nothing is due to her." For the wife is the genus: there are two kinds of wife; one being those mothers of a family which become wives by *coemptio*; the other kind are those which are only considered wives: and as Fabia was one of those last, it appears that nothing was bequeathed to her.

An argument is derived from similarity, in this way: "If those houses have fallen down, or got into disrepair, a life-interest in which is bequeathed to some one, the heir is not bound to restore or to repair them, any more than he is bound to replace a slave, if a slave, a life-interest in whom has been bequeathed to some one, has died."

An argument is derived from difference, thus: "It does not follow, if a man has bequeathed to his wife all the money which belonged to him, that therefore he bequeathed all which was down in his books as due to him; for there is a great difference whether the money is laid up in his strong box, or set down as due in his accounts."

An argument is derived from contraries, thus: "That woman to whom her husband has left a life-interest in all his property, has no right, if his cellars of wine and oil are left full, to think that they belong to her; for the use of them is what has been bequeathed to her, and not the misuse: and they are contrary to one another."

IV. An argument is derived from adjuncts, thus: "If a woman has made a will who has never given up her liberty by marriage, it does not appear that possession ought to be given by the edict of the praetor to the legatee under that will; for it is added, that in that case possession would seem proper to be given by that same edict, according to the wills of slaves, or exiles, or infants."

Arguments are derived from antecedents, and consequents, and contradictories, in this way. From antecedents: "If a divorce has been caused by the fault of the husband, although the woman has demanded it, still she is not bound to leave any of her dowry for her children."

From consequents: "If a woman having married a man with whom she had no right of intermarriage, has demanded a divorce, since the children who have been born do not follow their father, the father has no right to keep back any portion of the woman's dowry."

From contradictories: "If the head of a family has left to his wife in reversion after his son the life-interest in the female slaves, and has made no mention of any other reversionary heir, if the son dies, the woman shall not lose her life-interest. For that which has once been given to any one by will, cannot be taken away from the legatee to whom it has been given without his consent; for it is a contradiction for any one to have a right to receive a thing, and yet to be forced to give it up against his will."

An argument is derived from efficient causes, in this way: "All men have a right to add to a common party wall, a wall extending its whole length, either solid or on arches; but if any one in demolishing the common wall should promise to pay for any damages which may arise from his action, he will not be bound to pay for any damage sustained or caused by such arches: for the damage has been done, not by the party which demolished the common wall, but in consequence of some fault in the work, which was built in such a manner as to be unable to support itself."

An argument is derived from what has been done, in this way: "When a woman becomes the wife of a man, everything which has belonged to the woman now becomes the property of the husband under the name of dowry."

But in the way of comparison there are many kinds of valid arguments; in this way: "That which is valid in a greater affair, ought to be valid in a less: so that, if the law does not regulate the limits in the city, still more will it not compel any one to turn off the water in the city." Again, on the other hand: "Whatever is valid in a smaller matter ought to be valid also in a greater one. One may convert the preceding example." Also, "That which is valid in a parallel case ought to be valid in this which is a parallel case." As, "Since the usurpation of a farm depends on a term of two years, the law with respect to houses ought to be the same." But in the law houses are not mentioned, and so they are supposed to come under the same class as all other things, the property in which is determined by one year's use. Equity then must prevail, which requires similar laws in similar cases. [4]

[4] See chap. x.

But those arguments which are derived from external circumstances are deduced chiefly from authority. Therefore the Greeks call argumentations of that kind [Greek: *atechuoi*], that is, devoid of art. As if you were to answer in this way:—"In the case of some one building a roof for the purpose of covering a common wall, Publius Scaevola asserted that there was no right of carrying that roof so far that the water which ran off it should run on to any part of any building which did not belong to the owner of the roof. This I affirm to be law."

V. By these topics then which have been explained, a means of discovering and proving every sort of argument is supplied, as if they were elements of argument. Have we then said enough up to this point? I think we have, as far at least as you, an acute man and one deeply skilled in law, are concerned. But since I have to deal with a man who is very greedy when the feast in question is one of learning, I will prosecute the subject so that I will rather put forth something more than is necessary, than allow you to depart unsatisfied. As, then, each separate one of those topics which I have mentioned has its own proper members, I will follow them out as accurately as I can; and first of all I will speak of the definition itself.

Definition is a speech which explains that which is defined. But of definitions there are two principal kinds: one, of those things which exist; the other, of those which are understood. The things which I call existing are those which can be seen or touched; as a farm, a house, a wall, a gutter, a slave, an ox, furniture, provisions, and so on; of which kind of things some require at times to be defined by us. Those things, again, I say have no existence, which are incapable of being touched or proved, but which can be perceived by the mind and understood; as if you were to define usucaption, guardianship, nationality, or relationship; all, things which have no body, but which nevertheless have a certain conformation plainly marked out and impressed upon the mind, which I call the notion of them. They often require to be explained by definition while we are arguing about them.

And again, there are definitions by partition, and others by division: by partition, when the matter which is to be defined is separated, as it were, into different members; as if any one were to say that civil law was that which consists of laws, resolutions of the senate, precedents, the authority of lawyers, the edicts of magistrates, custom, and equity. But a definition by division embraces every form which comes under the entire genus which is defined; in this way: "Alienation is the surrender of anything which is a man's private property, or a legal cession of it to men who are able by law to avail themselves of such cession."

VI. There are also other kinds of definitions, but they have no connexion with the subject of this book; we have only got to say what is the manner of expressing a definition. This, then, is what the ancients prescribe: that when you have taken those things which are common to the thing which you wish to define with other things, you must pursue them till you make out of them altogether some peculiar property which cannot be transferred to anything else. As this: "An inheritance is money." Up to this point the definition is common, for there are many kinds of money. Add what follows: "which by somebody's death comes to some one else." It is not yet a definition, for money belonging to the dead can be possessed in many ways without inheritance. Add one word, "lawfully." By this time the matter will appear distinguished from general terms, so that the definition may stand thus:—"An inheritance is money which by somebody's death has lawfully come to some one else." It is not enough yet. Add, "without being either bequeathed by will, or held as some one else's property." The definition is complete. Again, take this:—"Those are *gentiles* who are of the same name as one another." That is insufficient. "And who are born of noble blood." Even that is not enough. "Who have never had any ancestor in the condition of a slave." Something is still wanting. "Who have never parted with their franchise." This, perhaps, may do. For I am not aware that Scaevola, the pontiff, added anything to this definition. And this principle holds good in each kind of definition, whether the thing to be defined is something which exists, or something which is understood.

VII. But we have shown now what is meant by partition, and by division. But it is necessary to explain more clearly wherein they differ. In partition, there are as it were members; as of a body—head, shoulders, hands, sides, legs, feet, and so on. In division there are forms which the Greeks call [Greek: *ideae*]; our countrymen who treat of such subjects call them species. And it is not a bad name, though it is an inconvenient one if we want to use it in different cases. For even if it were Latin to use such words, I should not like to say *specierum* and *speciebus*. And we have often occasion to use these cases. But I have no such objection to saying *formarum* and *formis*; and as the meaning of each word is the same, I do not think that convenience of sound is wholly to be neglected.

Men define genus and species or form in this manner:—"Genus is a notion relating to many differences. Species is a notion, the difference of which can be referred to the head and as it were fountain of the genus." I mean by notion that which the Greeks call sometimes [Greek: *ennoia*], and sometimes [Greek: *enoprolaepsis*]. It is knowledge implanted and previously acquired of each separate thing, but one which requires development. Species, then, are those forms into which genus is divided without any single one being omitted; as if any one were to divide justice into law, custom, and equity. A person who thinks that species are the same things as parts, is confounding the art; and being perplexed by some resemblance, he does not distinguish with sufficient acuteness what ought to be distinguished. Often, also, both orators and poets define by metaphor, relying on some verbal resemblance, and indeed not without giving a certain degree of pleasure. But I will not depart from your examples unless I am actually compelled to do so.

Aquillius, then, my colleague and intimate friend, was accustomed, when there was any discussion about shores, (all of which you lawyers insist upon it are public,) to define them to men who asked to whom that which was shore belonged, in this way: "Wherever the waves dashed;" that is, as if a man were to define youth as the flower of a man's age, or old age as the setting of life. Using a metaphor, he departs from the words proper to the matter in hand and to his own art. This is enough as to definition. Let us now consider the other points.

VIII. But we must employ partition in such a manner as to omit no part whatever. As if you wish to partition guardianship, you would act ignorantly if you were to omit any kind. But if you were partitioning off the different formulas of stipulations or judicial decisions, then it is not a fault to omit something in a matter which is of boundless extent. But in division it is a fault; for there is a settled number of species which are subordinate to each genus. The distribution of the parts is often more interminable still, like the drawing streams from a fountain. Therefore in the art of an orator, when the genus of a question is once laid down, the number of its species is added absolutely; but when rules are given concerning the embellishments of words and sentences, which are called [Greek: *schaemata*], the case is different; for the circumstances are more infinite: so that it may be understood from this also what the difference is which we assert to exist between partition and division. For although the words appear nearly equivalent to one another still, because the things are different, the expressions are also established as not synonymous to one another.

Many arguments are also derived from observation, and that is when they are deduced from the meaning of a word, which the Greeks call [Greek: *etumologia*]; or as we might translate it, word for word, *veriloquium*. But we, while avoiding the novel appearance of a word which is not very suitable, call this kind of argument *notatio*, because words are the *notes* by which we distinguish things. And therefore Aristotle calls the same source of argument [Greek: *sunbolou*], which is equivalent to the Latin *nota*. But when it is known what is meant we need not be so particular about the name. In a discussion then, many arguments are derived from words by means of observation; as when the question is asked, what is a *postliminium*—(I do not mean what are the objects to which this word applies, for that would be division, which is something of this sort: "*Postliminium* applies to a man, a ship, a mule with panniers, a horse, a mare who is accustomed to be bridled")—but when the meaning of the word itself, *postliminium*, is asked, and when the word itself is observed. And in this our countryman, Servius, as it seems, thinks that there is nothing to be observed except *post*, and he insists upon it that *liminium* is a mere extension of the word; as in *finitimus, legitimus, ceditimus,* timus has no more meaning than *tullius* has in *meditullius*.

But Scævola, the son of Publius Scævola, thinks the word is a compound one, so that it is made up of *post* and *limen.* So that those things which have been alienated from us, when they have come into the possession of our enemies, and, as it were, departed from their own threshold, then when they have returned behind that same threshold, appear to have returned *postliminio.* By which definition even the cause of Mancinus may be defended by saying that he returned *postliminio,*—that he was not surrendered, inasmuch as he was not received. For that no surrender and no gift can be understood to have taken place if there has been no reception of it.

IX. We next come to that topic which is derived from those things which are disposed in some way or other to that thing which is the subject of discussion. And I said just now that it was divided into many parts. And the first topic is derived from combination, which the Greeks call [Greek: *sizugia*], being a kindred thing to observation, which we have just been discussing, as, if we were only to understand that to be rain-water which we saw to have been collected from rain, Mucius would come, who, because the words *pluvia* and *pluendo* were akin, would say that all water ought to be kept out which had been increased by raining. But when an argument is derived from a genus, then it will not be necessary to trace it back to its origin, we may often stop on this side of that point, provided that which is deduced is higher than that for which it is deduced, as, "Rain water in its ultimate genus is that which descends from heaven and is increased by showers," but in reference to its more proximate sense, under which the right of keeping it off is comprised, the genus is, mischievous rain water. The subordinate species of that genus are waters which injure through a natural defect of the place, or those which are injurious on account of the works of man: for one of these kinds may be restrained by an arbitrator, but not the other.

Again, this argumentation is handled very advantageously, which is derived from a species when you pursue all the separate parts by tracing them back to the whole, in this way "If that is *dolus malus* when one thing is aimed at, and another pretended," we may enumerate the different modes in which that can be done, and then under some one of them we may range that which we are trying to prove has been done *dolo malo*. And that kind of argument is usually accounted one of the most irrefragable of all.

X. The next thing is similarity, which is a very extensive topic, but one more useful for orators and for philosophers than for men of your profession. For although all topics belong to every kind of discussion, so as to supply arguments for each, still they occurs more abundantly in discussions on some subjects, and more sparingly in others. Therefore the genera are known to you, but when you are to employ them the questions themselves will instruct you. For there are resemblances which by means of comparisons arrive at the point they aim at, in this manner. "If a guardian is bound to behave with good faith, and a partner, and any one to whom you have entrusted anything, and any one who has undertaken a trust then so ought an agent." This argument, arriving at the point at which it aims by a comparison of many instances, is called induction, which in Greek is called [Greek: *ipago*]. and it is the kind of argument which Socrates employed a great deal in his discourses.

Another kind of resemblance is obtained by comparison, when one thing is compared to some other single thing, and like to like, in this way "As if in any city there is a dispute as to boundaries because the boundaries of fields appear more extensive than those of cities, you may find it impossible to bring an arbitrator to settle the question of boundaries, so if rain water is injurious in a city, since the whole matter is one more for country magistrates, you may not be able to bring an arbitrator to settle the question of keeping off rain-water" Again, from the same topic of resemblance, examples are derived, as, "Crassus in Curius's trial used many examples, speaking of the man who by his will had appointed his heir in such a manner, that if he had had a son born within ten months of his death, and that son had died before coming into possession of the property held in trust for him, the revisionary heir would succeed to the inheritance. And the enumeration of precedents which Crassus brought forward prevailed". And you are accustomed to use this style of argument very frequently in replies. Even fictitious examples have all the force of real ones, but they belong rather to the orator than to you lawyers, although you also do use them sometimes, but in this way. "Suppose a man had given a slave a thing which a slave is by law incapable of receiving, is it on that account the act of the man who received it? or has he, who gave that present to his slave on that account taken any obligations on himself?" And in this kind of argument orators and philosophers are allowed to make even dumb things talk, so that the dead man be raised from the shades below, or that anything which intrinsically is absolutely impossible, may, for the sake of adding force to the argument, or diminishing, be spoken of as real and that figure is called hyperbole. And they may say other marvellous things, but theirs is a wider field. Still, out of the same topics, as I have said before, arguments are derived for the most important and the most trivial inquiries.

XI After similarity there follows difference between things, which is as different as possible from the preceding topic, still it is the same art which finds out resemblances and dissimilarities. These are instances of the same sort—"If you have contracted a debt to a woman, you can pay her without having recourse to a trustee, but what you owe to a minor, whether male or female; you cannot pay in the same manner."

The next topic is one which is derived from contraries. But the genera of contraries are several. One is of such things as differ in the same kind; as wisdom and jolly. But those things are said to be in the same kind, which, when they are proposed, are immediately met by certain contraries, as if placed opposite to them: as slowness is contrary to rapidity, and not weakness. From which contraries such arguments as these are deduced:—"If we avoid folly, let us pursue wisdom; and if we avoid wickedness, let us pursue goodness." These things, as they are contrary qualities in the same class, are called opposites. For there are other contraries, which we may call in Latin, *privantia*, and which the Greeks call [Greek: *steraetika*]. For the preposition *in* deprives the word of that force which it would have if *in* were not prefixed; as, "dignity, indignity—humanity, inhumanity," and other words of the same kind, the manner of dealing with which is the same as that of dealing with other kinds which I have called opposites. For there are also other kinds or contraries; as those which are compared to something or other; as, "twofold and simple; many and few; long and short; greater and less." There are also those very contrary things which are called negatives, which the Greeks call [Greek: *steraetika*]: as, "If this is the case, that is not." For what need is there for an instance? only let it be understood that in seeking for an argument it is not every contrary which is suitable to be opposed to another.

XII. But I gave a little while ago an instance drawn from adjuncts; showing that many things are added as accessories, which ought to be admitted, if we decided that possession ought to be given by the praetor's edict, in compliance with the will which that person made who had no right whatever to make a will. But this topic has more influence in conjectural causes, which are frequent in courts, of justice, when we are inquiring either what is, or what has been, or what is likely to be, or what possibly may happen. And the form of the topic itself is as follows. But this topic reminds us to inquire what happened before the transaction of which we are speaking, or at the same time with the transaction, or after the transaction. "This has nothing to do with the law, you had better apply to Cicero," our friend Gallus used to say, if any one brought him any cause which required an inquiry into matters of fact. But you will prefer that no topic of the art which I have begun to treat of should be omitted by me, lest if you should think that nothing was to be written here except what had reference to yourself, you should seem to be too selfish. This then is for the most part an oratorical topic; not only not much suited to lawyers, but not even to philosophers. For the circumstances which happened before the matter in question are inquired into, such as any preparation, any conferences, any place, any prearranged convivial meeting. And the circumstances which happened at the same time with the matter in question, are the noise of footfalls, the noise of men, the shadow of a body, or anything of that sort. The circumstances subsequent to the matter in question are, blushing, paleness, trepidation, or any other tokens of agitation or consciousness; and besides these, any such fact as a fire extinguished, a bloody sword, or any circumstance which can excite a suspicion of such an act.

XIII. The next topic is one peculiar to dialecticians; derived from consequents, and antecedents, and inconsistencies; and this one is very different from that drawn from differences. For adjuncts, of which we were speaking just now, do not always exist, but consequents do invariably. I call those things consequents which follow an action of necessity. And the same rule holds as to antecedents and inconsistencies; for whatever precedes each thing, that of necessity coheres with that theme; and whatever is inconsistent with it is of such a nature that it can never cohere with it. As then this topic is distributed in three divisions, into consequence, antecession, and inconsistency, there is one single topic to help us find the argument, but a threefold way of dealing with it. For what difference does it make, when you have once assumed that the ready money is due to the woman to whom all the money has been bequeathed, whether you conclude your argument in this way:—"If coined money is money, it has been bequeathed to the woman; but coined money is money; therefore it has been bequeathed to her;"—or in this way: "If ready money has not been bequeathed to her, then ready money is not money; but ready money is money; therefore it has been bequeathed to her;"—or in this way: "The cases of money not having been bequeathed, and of ready money not having been bequeathed, are identical; but money was bequeathed to her; therefore ready money was bequeathed to her?"

But the dialecticians call that conclusion of the argument in which, when you have first made an assumption, that which is connected with it follows as a consequence of the assumption, the first mood of the conclusion; and when, because you have denied the consequence, it follows that that also to which it was a consequence must be denied also, that is the second mood. But when you deny some things in combination, (and then another negation is added to them,) and from these things you assume something, so that what remains is also done away with, that is called the third mood of the conclusion. From this are derived those results of the rhetoricians drawn from contraries, which they call enthymemes. Not that every sentence may not be legitimately called an enthymeme; but, as Homer on account of his preeminence has appropriated the general name of poet to himself as his own among all the Greeks; so, though every sentence is an enthymeme, still, because that which is made up of contraries appears the most acute argument of the kind, that alone has possessed itself of the general name as its own peculiar distinction. Its kinds are these:—"Can you fear this man, and not fear that one?"—"You condemn this woman, against whom you bring no accusation; and do you say that this other one deserves punishment, whom you believe to deserve reward?"—"That which you do know is no good; that which you do not know is a great hindrance to you."

XIV. This kind of disputing is very closely connected with the mode of discussion adopted by you lawyers in reply, and still more closely with that adopted by philosophers, as they share with the orators in the employment of that general conclusion which is drawn from inconsistent sentences, which is called by dialecticians the third mood, and by rhetoricians an enthymeme. There are many other moods used by the rhetoricians, which consist of disjunctive propositions:—"Either this or that is the case; but this is the case; then that is not the case." And again:—"Either this or that is the case; but this is not the case; then that is the case." And these conclusions are valid, because in a disjunctive proposition only one alternative can be true. And from those conclusions which I have mentioned above, the former is called by the dialecticians the fourth mood, and the latter the fifth. Then they add a negation of conjunctive propositions; as, "It is not both this and that; but it is this; therefore it is not that." This is the sixth mood. The seventh is, "It is not both this and that; but it is not this; therefore it is that." From these moods innumerable conclusions are derived, in which nearly the whole science of dialectics consists. But even those which I have now explained are not necessary for this present discussion.

XV. The next topic is drawn from efficient circumstances which are called causes; and the next from the results produced by these efficient causes. I have already given instances of these, as of the other topics, and those too drawn from civil law; but these have a wider application.

There are then two kinds of causes; one which of its own force to a certainty produces that effect which is subordinate to it; as, "Fire burns;" the other is that which has no nature able to produce the effect in question, though still that effect cannot be produced without it; as, if any one were to say, that "brass was the cause of a statue;

because a statue cannot be made without it." Now of this kind of causes which are indispensable to a thing being done, some are quiet some passive, some, as it were, senseless; as, place, time, materials, tools, and other things of the same sort. But some exhibit a sort of preparatory process towards the production of the effect spoken of; and some of themselves do contribute some aid to it; although it is not indispensable; as meeting may have supplied the cause to love; love to crime. From this description of causes depending on one another in infinite series, is derived the doctrine of fate insisted on by the Stoics. And as I have thus divided the genera of causes, without which nothing can be effected, so also the genera of the efficient causes can be divided in the same manner. For there are some causes which manifestly produce the effect, without any assistance from any quarter; others which require external aid; as for instance, wisdom alone by herself makes men wise; but whether she is able alone to make men happy is a question.

XVI. Wherefore, when any cause efficient as to some particular end has inevitably presented itself in a discussion, it is allowable without any hesitation to conclude that what that cause must inevitably effect is effected. But when the cause is of such a nature that it does not inevitably effect the result, then the conclusion which follows is not inevitable And that description of causes which has an inevitable effect does not usually engender mistakes; but this description, without which a thing cannot take place, does often cause perplexity. For it does not follow, because sons cannot exist without parents, that there was therefore any unavoidable cause in the parents to have children. This, therefore, without which an effect cannot be produced, must be carefully separated from that by which it is certainly produced. For that is like—

> "Would that the lofty pine on Pelion's brow
> Had never fall'n beneath the woodman's axe!"

For if the beam of fir had never fallen to the ground, that Argo would not have been built; and yet there was not in the beams any unavoidably efficient power. But when

> "The fork'd and fiery bolt of Jove"

was hurled at Ajax's vessel, that ship was then inevitably burnt.

And again, there is a difference between causes, because some are such that without any particular eagerness of mind, without any expressed desire or opinion, they effect what is, as it were, their own work; as for instance, "that everything must die which has been born." But other results are effected either by some desire or agitation of mind, or by habit, or nature, or art, or chance. By desire, as in your case, when you read this book; by agitation, as in the case of any one who fears the ultimate issue of the present crisis; by habit, as in the case of a man who gets easily and rapidly in a passion; by nature, as vice increases every day; by art, as in the case of a man who paints well; by chance, as in the case of a man who has a prosperous voyage. None of these things are without some cause, and yet none of them are wholly owing to any single cause. But causes of this kind are not necessary ones.

XVII. But in some of these causes there is a uniform operation, and in others there is not. In nature and in art there is uniformity; but in the others there is none. But still of those causes which are not uniform, some are evident, others are concealed. Those are evident which touch the desire or judgment of the mind; those are concealed which are subject to fortune: for as nothing is done without some cause, this very obscure cause, which works in a concealed manner, is the issue of fortune. Again, these results which are produced are partly unintended, partly intentional. Those are unintended which are produced by necessity; those are intentional which are produced by design. But those results which are produced by fortune are either unintended or intentional. For to shoot an arrow is an act of intention; to hit a man whom you did not mean to hit is the result of fortune. And this is the topic which you use like a battering-ram in your forensic pleadings; if a weapon has flown from the man's hand rather than been thrown by him. Also agitation of mind may be divided into absence of knowledge and absence of intention. And although they are to a certain extent voluntary, (for they are diverted from their course by reproof or by admonition,) still they are liable to such emotions that even those acts of theirs which are intentional sometimes seem either unavoidable, or at all events unintentional.

The whole topic of these causes then being now fully explained, from their differences there is derived a great abundance of arguments in all the important discussions of orators and philosophers. And in the cases which you lawyers argue, if there is not so plentiful a stock, what there are, are perhaps more subtle and shrewd. For in private actions the decisions in the most important cases appear to me to depend a great deal on the acuteness of the lawyers. For they are constantly present, and are taken into counsel; and they supply weapons to able advocates whenever they have recourse to their professional wisdom.

In all those judicial proceedings then, in which the words "according to good faith" are added, or even those words, "as ought to be done by one good man to another;" and above all, in all cases of arbitration respecting matrimonial rights, in which the words "juster and better" occur, the lawyers ought to be always ready. For they know what "dishonest fraud," or "good faith," or "just," or "good" mean. They are acquainted with the law between partners; they know what the man who has the management of the affairs of another is bound to do with respect to him whose affairs he manages; they have laid down rules to show what the man who has committed a charge to another, and what he who has had it committed to him, ought to do; what a husband ought to confer on his wife, and a wife on her husband. It will, therefore, when they have by diligence arrived at a proper understanding of the topics from which the necessary arguments are derived, be in the power not only of orators and philosophers, but of lawyers also, to discuss with abundance of argument all the questions which can arise for their consideration.

XVIII. Conjoined to this topic of causes is that topic which is supplied by causes. For as cause indicates effect, so what has been effected points out what the efficient cause has been. This topic ordinarily supplies to orators and poets, and often to philosophers also, that is to say, to those who have an elegant and argumentative and rich style of eloquence, a wonderful store of arguments, when they predict what will result from each circumstance. For the knowledge of causes produces a knowledge of effects.

The remaining topic is that of comparison, the genus and instances of which have been already explained, as they have in the case of the other topics. At present we must explain the manner of dealing with this one. Those things then are compared which are greater than one another, or less than one another, or equal to one another. In which these points are regarded; number, appearance, power, and some particular relation to some particular thing.

Things will be compared in number thus: so that more advantages may be preferred to fewer; fewer evils to more; more lasting advantages to those which are more short-lived; those which have an extensive application to those the effect of which is narrowed: those from which still further advantages may be derived, and those which many people may imitate and reproduce.

Things again will be compared with reference to their appearance, so that those things may be preferred which are to be desired for their own sake, to those which are only sought for the sake of something else: and so that innate and inherent advantages may be preferred to acquired and adventitious ones; complete good to mixed good; pleasant things to things less pleasant; honourable things to such as are merely useful; easy things to difficult ones; necessary to unnecessary things; one's own advantage to that of others; rare things to common ones; desirable things to those which you can easily do without; things complete to things which are only begun; wholes to parts; things proceeding on reason to things void of reason; voluntary to necessary things; animate to inanimate things; things natural to things not natural; things skilfully produced by art to things with which art has no connexion.

But power in a comparison is perceived in this way: an efficient cause is more important than one which effects nothing; those causes which can act by themselves are superior to those which stand in need of the aid of others; those which are in our power are preferable to those which are in the power of another; lasting causes surpass those which are uncertain; things of which no one can deprive us are better than things which can be easily taken away.

But the way in which people or things are disposed towards some things is of this sort: the interests of the chief citizens are more important than those of the rest: and also, those things which are more agreeable, which are approved of by more people, or which are praised by the most virtuous men, are preferable. And as in a comparison these things are the better, so those which are contrary to them are the worse.

But the comparison between things like or equal to each other has no elation or submission; for it is on equal terms: but there are many things which are compared on account of their very equality; which are usually concluded in this manner: "If to assist one's fellow-citizens with counsel and personal aid deserves equal praise, those men who act as counsellors ought to enjoy an equal glory with those who are the actual defenders of a state." But the first premiss is certainly the case; therefore so must the consequent be.

Every rule necessary for the discovery of arguments is now concluded; so that as you have proceeded from definition, from partition, from observation, from words connected with one another, from genus, from species, from similarity, from difference, from contraries, from accessories, from consequents, from antecedents, from things inconsistent with one another, from causes, from effects, from a comparison with greater, or lesser, or equal things,—there is no topic of argument whatever remaining to be discovered.

XIX. But since we originally divided the inquiry in such a way that we said that other topics also were contained in the very matter which was the subject of inquiry; (but of those we have spoken at sufficient length:) that others were derived from external subjects; and of these we will say a little; although those things have no relation whatever to your discussions. But still we may as well make the thing complete, since we have begun it. Nor are you a man who take no delight in anything except civil law; and since this treatise is dedicated to you, though not so exclusively but that it will also come into the hands of other people, we must take pains to be as serviceable as possible to those men who are addicted to laudable pursuits.

This sort of argumentation then which is said not to be founded on art, depends on testimony. But we call everything testimony which is deduced from any external circumstances for the purpose of implanting belief. Now it is not every one who is of sufficient weight to give valid testimony; for authority is requisite to make us believe things. But it is either a man's natural character or his age which invests him with authority. The authority derived from a man's natural character depends chiefly on his virtue; but on his age there are many things which confer authority; genius, power, fortune, skill, experience, necessity, and sometimes even a concourse of accidental circumstances. For men think able and opulent men, and men who have been esteemed during a long period of their lives, worthy of being believed Perhaps they are not always right; but still it is not easy to change the sentiments of the common people; and both those who form judgments and those who adopt vague opinions shape everything with reference to them. For those men who are eminent for those qualities which I have mentioned, seem to be eminent for virtue itself. But in the other circumstances also which I have just enumerated, although there is in them no appearance of virtue, still sometimes belief is confirmed by them, if either any skill is displayed,—for the influence of knowledge in inspiring belief is very great; or any experience—for people are apt to believe those who are men of experience.

XX. Necessity also engenders belief, which sways both bodies and minds. For what men say when worn out with tortures, and stripes, and fire, appears to be uttered by truth itself. And those statements which proceed from agitation of mind, such as pain, cupidity, passion, and fear, because those feelings have the force of necessity, bring authority and belief. And of this kind are those circumstances from which at times the truth is discovered; childhood, sleep, ignorance, drunkenness, insanity. For children have often indicated something, though ignorant to what it related; and many things have often been discovered by sleep, and wine, and insanity. Many men also have without knowing it fallen into great difficulties, as lately happened to Stalenus; who said things in the hearing of certain excellent men, though a wall was between them, which, when they were revealed and brought before a judicial tribunal, were thought so wicked that he was rightly convicted of a capital offence. And we have heard something similar concerning Pausanias the Lacedæmonian.

But the concourse of fortuitous events is often of this kind; when anything has happened by chance to interrupt, when anything was being done or said which it was desirable should not have been done or said. Of this kind is that multitude of suspicions of treason which were heaped upon Palamedes. And circumstances of this kind are sometimes scarcely able to be refuted by truth itself. Of this kind too is ordinary report among the common people; which is as it were the testimony of the multitude.

But those things which create belief on account of the virtue of the witness are of a two-fold kind; one of which is valid on account of nature, the other by industry. For the virtue of the gods is eminent by nature; but that of men, because of their industry.

Testimonies of this kind are nearly divine, first of all, that of oration, (for oracles were so called from that very same word, as there is in them the oration of the gods;) then that of things in which there are, as it were, many divine works; first of all, the word itself, and its whole order and ornaments; then the airy flights and songs of birds; then the sound and heat of that same air; and the numerous prodigies of divers kinds seen on the earth; and also, the power of foreseeing the future by means of the entrails of victims: many things, too, which are shown to the living by those who are asleep: from all which topics the testimonies of the gods are at times adduced so as to create belief.

In the case of a man, the opinion of his virtue is of the greatest weight. For opinion goes to this extent, that those men have virtue, not only who do really possess it, but those also who appear to possess it. Therefore, those men whom they see endowed with genius and diligence and learning, and whose life they see is consistent and approved of, like Cato and Lælius, and Scipio, and many others, they consider such men as they themselves would wish to be. And not only do they think them such who enjoy honours conferred on them by the people, and who busy themselves with affairs of state, but also those who are orators, and philosophers, and poets, and historians; from whose sayings and writings authority is often sought for to establish belief.

XXI. Having thus explained all the topics serviceable for arguing, the first thing to be understood is, that there is no discussion whatever to which some topic or other is not applicable; and on the other hand, that it is not every topic which is applicable to every discussion; but that different topics are suited to different subjects.

There are two kinds of inquiry: one, infinite; the other, definite. The definite one is that which the Greeks call [Greek: *hupothesis*], and we, a cause; the infinite one, that which they call [Greek: *thesis*], and which we may properly term a proposition.

A cause is determined by certain persons, places, times, actions, and things, either all or most of them; but a proposition is declared in some one of those things, or in several of them, and those not the most important: therefore, a proposition is a part of a cause. But the whole inquiry is about some particular one of those things in which causes are contained; whether it be one, or many, or sometimes all. But of inquiries, concerning whatever thing they are, there two kinds; one theoretical, the other practical. Theoretical inquiries are those of which the proposed aim is science; as, 'If it is inquired whether right proceeds from nature, or from some covenant, as it were, and bargain between men. But the following are instances of practical inquiry: "Whether it is the part of a wise man to meddle with statesmanship." The inquiries into theoretical matters are threefold; as what is inquired is, whether a thing exists, or what it is, or what its character is. The first of these queries is explained by conjecture; the second, by definition; the third, by distinctions of right and wrong.

The method of conjecture is distributed into four parts; one of which is, when the inquiry is whether something exists; a second, when the question is, whence it has originated; a third, when one seeks to know what cause produced it; the fourth is that in which the alterations to which the subject is liable are examined: "Whether it exists or not; whether there is anything honourable, anything intrinsically and really just; or whether these things only exist in opinion." But the inquiry whence it has originated, is when an inquiry is such as this, "Whether virtue is implanted by nature, or whether it can be engendered by instruction." But the efficient cause is like this, as when an inquiry is, "By what means eloquence is produced." Concerning the alterations of anything, in this manner: "Whether eloquence can by any alteration be converted into a want of eloquence."

XXII. But when the question is what a thing is; the notion is to be explained, and the property, and the division, and the partition. For these things are all attributed to definition. Description also is added, which the Greeks call [Greek: *charaktaer*]. A notion is inquired into in this way: "Whether that is just which is useful to that person who is the more powerful." Property, in this way: "Whether melancholy is incidental to man alone, or whether beasts also are liable to it." Division, and also partition, in this manner: "Whether there are three descriptions of good things." Description, like this: "What sort of person a miser is; what sort of person a flatterer;" and other things of that sort, by which the nature and life of a man are described.

But when the inquiry is what the character of something is, the inquiry is conducted either simply, or by way of comparison. Simply, in this way: "Whether glory is to be sought for." By way of comparison, in this way: "Whether glory is to be preferred to riches." Of simple inquiries there are three kinds; about seeking for or avoiding anything, about the right and the wrong; about what is honourable and what is discreditable. But of inquiries by way of comparison there are two; one of the thing itself and something else; one of something greater and something else. Of seeking for and avoiding a thing, in this way: "Whether riches are to be sought for: whether poverty is to be avoided." Concerning right and wrong: "Whether it is right to revenge oneself, whoever the person may be from whom one has received an injury." Concerning what is honourable and what is discreditable: "Whether it is honourable to die for one's country." But of the other kind of inquiry, which has been stated to be twofold, one is about the thing in question and something else; as if it were asked, "What is the difference between a friend and a flatterer, between a king and a tyrant?" The other is between something greater and something less; as if it were asked, "Whether eloquence is of more consequence than the knowledge of civil law." And this is enough about theoretical inquiries.

It remains to speak of practical ones; of which there are two kinds: one relating to one's duty, the other to engendering, or calming, or utterly removing any affection of the mind. Relating to duty thus: as when the question is, "Whether children ought to be bad." Relating to influencing the mind, when exhortations are delivered to men to defend the republic, or when they are encouraged to seek glory and praise: of which kind of addresses are complaints, and encouragements, and tearful commiseration; and again, speeches extinguishing anger, or at other times removing fear, or repressing the exultation of joy, or effacing melancholy. As these different divisions belong to general inquiries, they are also transferable to causes.

XXIII. But the next thing to be inquired is, what topics are adapted to each kind of inquiry; for all those which we have already mentioned are suitable to most kinds; but still, different topics, as I have said before, are better suited to different investigations. Those arguments are the most suitable to conjectural discussion which can be deduced from causes, from effects, or from dependent circumstances. But when we have need of definition, then we must have recourse to the principles and science of defining. And akin to this is that other argument also which we said was employed with respect to the subject in question and something else; and that is a species of definition. For if the question is, "Whether pertinacity and perseverance are the same thing," it must be decided by definitions. And the topics which are incidental to a discussion of this kind are those drawn from consequents, or antecedents, or inconsistencies, with the addition also of those two topics which are deduced from causes and effects. For if such and such a thing is a consequence of this, but not a consequence of that; or if such and such a thing is a necessary antecedent to this, but not to that; or if it is inconsistent with this, but not with that; or if one thing is the cause of this, and another the cause of that; or if this is effected by one thing, and that by another thing; from any one of these topics it may be discovered whether the thing which is the subject of discussion is the same thing or something else.

With respect to the third kind of inquiry, in which the question is what the character of the matter in question is, those things are incidental to the comparison which were enumerated just now under the topic of comparison. But in that kind of inquiry where the question is about what is to be sought for or avoided, those arguments are employed which refer to advantages or disadvantages, whether affecting the mind or body, or being external. And again, when the inquiry is not what is honourable or discreditable, all our argument must be addressed to the good or bad qualities of the mind.

But when right and wrong are being discussed, all the topics of equity are collected. These are divided in a two-fold manner, as to whether they are such by nature or owing to institutions. Nature has two parts to perform, to defend itself, and to indicate right. But the agreements which establish equity are of a threefold character: one part is that which rests on laws; one depends on convenience; the third is founded on and established by antiquity of custom. And again, equity itself is said to be of a threefold nature: one division of it having reference to the gods above; another, to the shades below; a third, to mankind. The first is called piety; the second, sanctity; the third, justice or equity.

XXIV. I have said enough about propositions. There are now a few things which require to be said about causes. For they have many things in common with propositions.

There are then three kinds of causes; having for their respective objects, judgment, deliberation, and panegyric. And the object of each points out what topics we ought to employ in each. For the object of judicial judgment is right; from which also it derives its name. And the divisions of right were explained when we explained the divisions of equity. The object of deliberation is utility; of which the divisions have also been already explained when we were treating of things to be desired. The object of panegyric is honour; concerning which also we have already spoken.

But inquiries which are definite are all of them furnished with appropriate topics, as if they belonged to themselves, being divided into accusation and defence. And in them there are these kinds of argumentation. The accuser accuses a person of an act; the advocate for the defence opposes one of these excuses: either that the thing imputed has not been done; or that, if it has been done, it deserves to be called by a different name; or that it was done lawfully and rightly. Therefore, the first is called a defence either by way of denial or by way of conjecture; the second is called a defence by definition; the third, although it is an unpopular name, is called the judicial one.

XXV. The arguments proper to these excuses, being derived from the topics which we have already set forth, have been explained in our oratorical rules. But the refutation of an accusation, in which there is a repelling of a charge, which is called in Greek [Greek: *stasis*], is in Latin called *status*. On which there is founded, in the first place, such a defence as may effectually resist the attack. And also, in the deliberations and panegyrics the same refutations often have place. For it is often denied that those things are likely to happen which have been stated by some or other in his speech as sure to take place; if it can be shown either that they are actually impossible, or that they cannot be brought about without extreme difficulty. And in this kind of argumentation the conjectural refutation takes place. But when there is any discussion about utility, or honour, or equity, and about those things which are contrary to one another, then come in denials, either of the law or of the name of the action. And the same is the case in panegyrics. For one may either deny that that has been done which the person is praised for; or else that it ought to bear that name which the praiser has conferred on it, or else one may altogether deny that it deserves any praise at all, as not having been done rightly or lawfully. And Caesar employed all these different kinds of denial with exceeding impudence when speaking against my friend Cato. But the contest which arises from a denial is called by the Greeks [Greek: *krinomenon*]; I, while writing to you, prefer calling it "the precise point in dispute." But for the parts within which this discussion on the point in dispute is contained, they may be called the containing parts; being as it were the foundations of the defence; and if they are taken away there would be no defence at all. But since in arguing controversies there ought to be nothing which has more weight than the law itself, we must take pains to have the law as our assistant and witness. And in this there are, as it were, other new denials, which are called legitimate subjects of discussion. For then it is urged in defence, that the law does not say what the adversary states it to say, but something else. And that happens when the terms of the law are ambiguous, so that they can be understood in two different senses. Then the intention of the framer is opposed to the letter of the law; so that the question is, whether the words or the intention ought to have the greatest validity? Then again, another law is adduced contrary to this law. So there are three kinds of doubts which can give rise to a dispute with respect to every written document; ambiguity of expression, discrepancy between the expression and the intention, and also written documents opposed to the one in question. For this is evident; that these kinds of disputes are no more incidental to laws than to wills, or covenants, or to anything else which is contained in writing. And the way to treat these topics is explained in other books.

XXVI. Nor is it only entire pleadings which are assisted by these topics, but the same are useful in the separate parts of an orator; being partly peculiar and partly general. As in the opening of a speech, in which the orator must employ peculiar topics in order to render his hearers well disposed to him, and docile, and attentive. And also he must attend to his relations of facts, so that they may have a bearing on his object, that is to say, that they may be plain, and brief, and intelligible, and credible, and respectable, and dignified: for although these qualities ought to be apparent throughout the whole speech, still they are peculiarly necessary in any narration. But since the belief which is given to a narration is engendered by persuasiveness, we have already, in the treatises which we have written on the general subject of oratory, explained what topics they are which have the greatest power to persuade the hearers. But the peroration has other points to attend to, and especially amplification; the effect of which ought to be, that the mind of the hearer is agitated or tranquillized by it; and if it has already been affected in that way, that the whole speech shall either increase its agitation, or calm it more completely.

For this kind of peroration, by which pity, and anger, and hatred, and envy, and similar feelings of the mind are excited, rules are furnished in those books, which you may read over with me whenever you like. But as to the point on which I have known you to be anxious, your desires ought now to be abundantly satisfied. For, in order not to pass over anything which had reference to the discovery of arguments in every sort of discussion, I have embraced more topics than were desired by you; and I have done as liberal sellers often do, when they have sold a house or a farm, the movables being all excepted from the sale, still give some of them to the purchaser, which appear to be well placed as ornaments or conveniences. And so we have chosen to throw in some ornaments that were not strictly your due, in addition to that with which we had bound ourselves to furnish you.

* * * * *

THE END

Breinigsville, PA USA
25 August 2010
244209BV00001B/83/P